THE ENCYCLOPEDIA OF PSYCHOACTIVE DRUGS

S E R I E S 1

S E R I E S 2

THE ADDICTIVE PERSONALITY

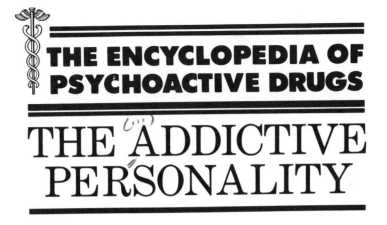

THE ENCYCLOPEDIA OF PSYCHOACTIVE DRUGS

THE ADDICTIVE PERSONALITY

W. MILES COX, Ph.D.

University of Minnesota

LEARNING RESOURCE CENTER
CHARLES CHELSEA HOUSE PUBLISHERS TY COLLEGE
NEW YORK   PHILADELPHIA
LA PLATA, MARYLAND

COVER: *La Morphinomane,* from Victor Arwas, *Berthon and Grassset,* London: Academy Editions, 1978.

Chelsea House Publishers

EDITOR-IN-CHIEF: Remmel Nunn
MANAGING EDITOR: Karyn Gullen Browne
PICTURE EDITOR: Adrian G. Allen
ART DIRECTOR: Maria Epes
MANUFACTURING DIRECTOR: Gerald Levine
SYSTEMS MANAGER: Lindsey Ottman
PRODUCTION MANAGER: Joseph Romano

THE ENCYCLOPEDIA OF PSYCHOACTIVE DRUGS

EDITOR OF UPDATED MATERIAL: Ann Keene

STAFF FOR THE ADDICTIVE PERSONALITY

PRODUCTION EDITOR: Marie Claire Cebrián
LAYOUT: Bernard Schleifer
APPENDIXES AND TABLES: Gary Tong
PICTURE RESEARCH: Elizabeth Terhune, Tamara Fulop, Toby Greenberg

Library of Congress Cataloging in Publication Data
Cox, W. Miles.
   The addictive personality.
   (The Encyclopedia of psychoactive drugs)
   Bibliography: p.
   Includes index.
   Summary: Examines the personality of the drug addict to determine if there are
characteristic traits before as well as after addiction takes place.
   1. Drug Abuse—Psychological aspects—Juvenile literature.   2. Personality—
Juvenile literature.   [1. Drug abuse—Psychological aspects.   2. Personality]
I. Title.   II. Series.
RC564.C695   1986   616.86'3   86-988
ISBN 0-87754-773-4
   0-7910-0751-0 (pbk.)

CONTENTS

The game of roulette is played in many casinos. Although gambling is socially acceptable, it can become addictive; chronic gamblers, like some drug abusers, are victims of their own psychological craving.

FOREWORD

Since the 1960s, the abuse of psychoactive substances—drugs that alter mood and behavior—has grown alarmingly. Many experts in the fields of medicine, public health, law enforcement, and crime prevention are calling the situation an epidemic. Some legal psychoactive substances—alcohol, caffeine, and nicotine, for example—have been in use since colonial times; illegal ones such as heroin and marijuana have been used to a varying extent by certain segments of the population for decades. But only in the late 20th century has there been widespread reliance on such a variety of mind-altering substances—by youth as well as by adults.

Day after day, newspapers, magazines, and television and radio programs bring us the grim consequences of this dependence. Addiction threatens not only personal health but the stability of our communities and currently costs society an estimated $180 billion annually in the United States alone. Drug-related violent crime and death are increasingly becoming a way of life in many of our cities, towns, and rural areas alike.

Why do people use drugs of any kind? There is one simple answer: to "feel better," physically or mentally. The antibiotics your doctor prescribes for an ear infection destroy the bacteria and make the pain go away. Aspirin can make us more comfortable by reducing fever, banishing a headache, or relieving joint pain from arthritis. Cigarettes put smokers at ease in social situations; a beer or a cocktail helps a worker relax after a hard day on the job. Caffeine, the most widely used drug in America, wakes us up in the morning and overcomes fatigue when we have exams to study for or a long drive to make. Prescription drugs, over-the-counter remedies, tobacco products, alcoholic beverages, caffeine products—all of these are legally available substances that have the capacity to change the way we feel.

But the drugs causing the most concern today are not found in a package of NoDoz or in an aspirin bottle. The drugs that government and private agencies are spending billions of dollars to overcome in the name of crime prevention, law enforcement, rehabilitation, and education have names like crack, angel dust, pot, horse, and speed. Cocaine, PCP, marijuana, heroin, and amphetamines can be very dangerous indeed, to both users and those with whom they live, go to school, and work. But other mood- and mind-altering substances are having a devastating impact, too—especially on youth.

Consider alcohol: The minimum legal drinking age in all 50 states is now 21, but adolescent consumption remains high, even as a decline in other forms of drug use is reported. A recent survey of high school seniors reveals that on any given weekend one in three seniors will be drunk; more than half of all high school seniors report that they have driven while they were drunk. The average age at which a child has his or her first drink is now 12, and more than 1 in 3 eighth-graders report having been drunk at least once.

Or consider nicotine, the psychoactive and addictive ingredient of tobacco: While smoking has declined in the population as a whole, the number of adolescent girls who smoke has been steadily increasing. Because certain health hazards of smoking have been conclusively demonstrated—its relationship to heart disease, lung cancer, and respiratory disease; its link to premature birth and low birth weight of babies whose mothers smoked during pregnancy—the long-term effects of such a trend are a cause for concern.

Studies have shown that almost all drug abuse begins in the preteen and teenage years. It is not difficult to understand why: Adolescence is a time of tremendous change and turmoil, when teenagers face the tasks of discovering their identity, clarifying their sexual roles, asserting their independence as they learn to cope with authority, and searching for goals. The pressures—from friends, parents, teachers, coaches, and one's own self—are great, and the temptation to want to "feel better" by taking drugs is powerful.

Psychoactive drugs are everywhere in our society, and their use and misuse show no sign of waning. The lack of success in the so-called war on drugs, begun in earnest in the 1980s, has shown us that we cannot "drug proof" our homes, schools, workplaces, and communities. What we can do, however, is make available the latest information on these substances and their effects and ask that those reading it consider the information carefully.

The newly updated ENCYCLOPEDIA OF PSYCHOACTIVE DRUGS, specifically written for young people, provides up-to-date information on a variety of substances that are widely abused in today's society. Each volume is devoted to a specific substance or pattern of abuse and is designed to answer the questions that young readers are likely to ask about drugs. An individualized glossary in each volume defines key words and terms, and newly enlarged and updated appendixes include recent statistical data as well as a special section on AIDS and its relation to drug abuse. The editors of the ENCYCLOPEDIA OF PSYCHOACTIVE DRUGS hope this series will help today's adolescents make intelligent choices as they prepare for maturity in the 21st century.

Ann Keene, Editor

People crowd into a bar in Washington, D.C. Although in moderation alcohol can relieve tension and anxiety, people sometimes come to rely on its effects, a habit that can lead to addiction.

USES AND ABUSES

JACK H. MENDELSON, M.D.
NANCY K. MELLO, Ph.D.
Alcohol and Drug Abuse Research Center
Harvard Medical School—McLean Hospital

*H*uman beings are endowed with the gift of wizardry, a talent for discovery and invention. The discovery and invention of substances that change the way we feel and behave are among our special accomplishments, and like so many other products of our wizardry, these substances have the capacity to harm as well as to help.

Consider alcohol—available to all and recognized as both harmful and pleasure inducing since biblical times. The use of alcoholic beverages dates back to our earliest ancestors. Alcohol use and misuse became associated with the worship of gods and demons. One of the most powerful Greek gods was Dionysus, lord of fruitfulness and god of wine. The Romans adopted Dionysus but changed his name to Bacchus. Festivals and holidays associated with Bacchus celebrated the harvest and the origins of life. Time has blurred the images of the Bacchanalian festival, but the theme of drunkenness as a major part of celebration has survived the pagan gods and remains a familiar part of modern society. The term *Bacchanalian festival* conveys a more appealing image than "drunken orgy" or "pot party," but whatever the label, some of the celebrants will inevitably start up the "high" escalator to the next plateau. Once there, the de-escalation is often difficult.

According to reliable estimates, 1 out of every 10 Americans develops a serious alcohol-related problem sometime in his or her lifetime. In addition, automobile accidents caused by drunken drivers claim the lives of more than 20,000 people each year, and injure 25 times that number. Many of the victims are gifted young people just starting out in adult life. Hospital emergency rooms abound with patients seeking help for alcohol-related injuries.

Who is to blame? Can we blame the many manufacturers who produce such an amazing variety of alcoholic beverages? Should we blame the educators who fail to explain the perils of intoxication or so exaggerate the dangers of drinking that no one could possibly believe them? Are friends to blame— those peers who urge others to "drink more and faster," or the macho types who stress the importance of being able to "hold your liquor?" Casting blame, however, is hardly constructive, and pointing the finger is a fruitless way to deal with problems. Alcoholism and drug abuse have few culprits but many victims. Accountability begins with each of us, every time we choose to use or to misuse an intoxicating substance.

It is ironic that some of our earliest medicines, derived from natural plant products, are used today to poison and to intoxicate. Relief from pain and suffering is one of society's many continuing goals. More than 3,000 years ago, the Therapeutic Papyrus of Thebes, one of our earliest written records, gave instructions for the use of opium in the treatment of pain. Opium, in the form of its major derivative, morphine, remains one of the most powerful drugs we have for pain relief. But opium, morphine, and similar compounds, such as heroin, have also been used by many to induce changes in mood and feeling. Another example of a natural substance that has been misused is the coca leaf, which for centuries was used by the Indians of Peru to reduce fatigue and hunger. Its modern derivative, cocaine, has important medical use as a local anesthetic. Unfortunately, its increasing abuse in recent years has reached epidemic proportions.

The purpose of this series is to provide information about the nature and behavioral effects of alcohol and drugs and the probable consequences of their use. The authors believe that up-to-date, objective information about alcohol and drugs will help readers make better decisions about the wisdom of their use. The information presented here (and in other books in this series) is based on many clinical and laboratory studies and observations by people from diverse walks of life.

Over the centuries, novelists, poets, and dramatists have provided us with many insights into the effects of alcohol and drug use. Physicians, lawyers, biologists, psychologists, and social scientists have contributed to a better understanding of the causes and consequences of using these substances. The authors in this series have attempted to gather and condense all the latest information about drug use. They have also described the sometimes wide gaps in our knowledge and have suggested some new ways to answer many difficult questions.

How, for example, do alcohol and drug problems get started? And what is the best way to treat them when they do? Not too many years ago, alcoholics and drug abusers were regarded as evil, immoral, or both. Many now believe that these persons suffer from very complicated diseases involving deep psychological and social problems. To understand how the disease begins and progresses, it is necessary to understand the nature of the substance, the behavior of the afflicted person, and the characteristics of the society or culture in which that person lives.

The diagram below shows the interaction of these three factors. The arrows indicate that the substance not only affects the user personally but the society as well. Society influences attitudes toward the substance, which in turn affect its availability. The substance's impact upon the society may support or discourage the use and abuse of that substance.

SUBSTANCE
(ALCOHOL OR DRUG)

PERSON ←——————→ SOCIETY

Although many of the social environments we live in are very similar, some of the most subtle differences can strongly influence our thinking and behavior. Where we live, go to school and work, whom we discuss things with—all influence our opinions about drug use. Yet we also share certain commonly accepted beliefs that outweigh any differences in our attitudes. The authors in this series have tried to identify and discuss the central, most crucial issues concerning drug use.

A pub sign in Great Britain. Drinking alcohol, which is often engaged in for social purposes, can in excess actually cause antisocial, aggressive, and violent behavior.

Regrettably, human wizardry in developing new substances in medical therapeutics has not always been paralleled by intelligent usage. Although we do know a great deal about the effects of alcohol and drugs, we have yet to learn how to impart that knowledge, especially to young adults.

Does it matter? What harm does it do to smoke a little pot or have a few beers? What is it like to be intoxicated? How long does it last? Will it make me feel really fine? Will it make me sick? What are the risks? These are but a few of the questions answered in this series, which we hope will enable the reader to make wise decisions concerning the crucial issue of drugs.

Information sensibly acted upon can go a long way toward helping everyone develop his or her best self. As one keen and sensitive observer, Dr. Lewis Thomas, has said,

> *There is nothing at all absurd about the human condition. We matter. It seems to me a good guess, hazarded by a good many people who have thought about it, that we may be engaged in the formation of something like a mind for the life of this planet. If this is so, we are still at the most primitive stage, still fumbling with language and thinking, but infinitely capacitated for the future. Looked at this way, it is remarkable that we've come as far as we have in so short a period, really no time at all as geologists measure time. We are the newest, the youngest, and the brightest thing around.*

A young woman studies her figure critically in a mirror. A compulsive fear of obesity is a characteristic of anorexia nervosa, an eating disorder increasingly common among adolescent females that can cause severe health problems and even death.

CHAPTER 1

PERSONALITY AND ADDICTIVE BEHAVIOR

*T*he use of psychoactive (mood-altering) substances is as ancient as humanity. Through the ages people have turned to distilled spirits, opiates, and other natural or synthetic drugs in search of relief from boredom, depression, and anxiety—or simply to get "high."

But despite the fact that the use of psychoactive substances is present to varying degrees in many societies, incidences of severe habit formation or addiction occur among only a small percentage of those who expose themselves to these substances. To gauge the true measure of addiction, we can look at how far a user will go to get a particular drug, determine to what extent use of this drug dominates his or her life and values, and judge how much control a user has over the abused substance. When drug use or any other compulsive behavior becomes the center of a person's existence, becoming more important than all other aspects of his or her life, we can then say that such a person is to all intents and purposes "addicted."

Although the concept of an "addictive personality" is still a controversial one, researchers are becoming increasingly convinced that certain types of people are more prone to addictive behavior than others. Experts in the field of drug and alcohol abuse have put forth various theories and explanations as to why, for example, some people can drink quite heavily without becoming truly addicted, while others, who may in fact drink less alcohol, slide down the road of abuse from heavy "problem" drinking into alcoholism.

Current research into the nature of alcoholism, for example, attributes the disease to a number of factors. Physiological causes may be partially responsible for the excessive use of alcohol by some people. In other words, a person may have a biochemical makeup that causes his or her initial experiences with a particular substance to be more euphoric than a "normal" person's would be. Genetic factors also seem to play a part in making some people more prone to alco-

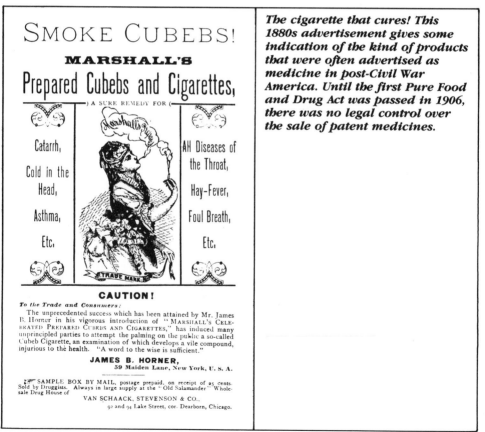

The cigarette that cures! This 1880s advertisement gives some indication of the kind of products that were often advertised as medicine in post-Civil War America. Until the first Pure Food and Drug Act was passed in 1906, there was no legal control over the sale of patent medicines.

holism than others. In fact, some studies have shown that children born to alcoholic parents but raised apart from them still frequently become alcoholics.

The causes of alcoholism and other addictions are various and complex. However, psychologists who administer personality tests to addicted individuals have found that these individuals have distinctive personality traits—whatever their origin—that distinguish them from other people. In some cases, the personality traits precede the addiction; in others, they seem to be caused by the addiction. Laboratory studies of people considered most likely to develop problems with alcohol and anecdotal descriptions by alcoholics of their initial drinking experiences indicate that initially alcohol has strong, positive effects on the personalities of these people. However, the long-range effects of excessive use of alcohol on personality are consistently negative.

What, exactly, do we mean by *addictive behavior*? Broadly speaking, behavior is labeled addictive when it is excessive, compulsive, beyond the control of the person who engages in it, and destructive psychologically or physically.

Addictive behavior usually involves the excessive use of psychoactive drugs, such as alcohol, heroin, cocaine, marijuana, nicotine, or even caffeine. However, major eating disorders—such as anorexia and bulimia—are also forms of addictive behavior, as are excessive gambling, exercising, and television watching.

Most psychoactive drugs either stimulate or depress the central nervous system. Stimulant drugs keep people awake and alert, increase their energy, and lift their spirits. Depressant drugs slow people down, help them to tune out unpleasant thoughts and events, and calm their tensions and anxieties. Some examples of stimulant drugs are caffeine, cocaine, and amphetamines. Some examples of depressant drugs are alcohol, narcotics, and tranquilizers.

Defining the Characteristics of Addictive Behavior

Two basic reactions occur when people take psychoactive drugs regularly—tolerance and dependence. These reactions are the essential characteristics of addictive behavior and are central to an understanding of it.

By *tolerance* we mean that as people continue over a period of time to use a given amount of a psychoactive drug, the drug comes to have less and less of an effect on them. As the central nervous system adapts to the drug, a user requires larger and larger doses to achieve the same effect. The phenomenon of tolerance is believed to result from natural reactions of the body. The body reacts as if it "knows" that the drug is a foreign substance, and so sets up defenses to counteract the effects of the drug.

Dependence—which may be psychological and/or physical—indicates a need for a particular substance or activity so severe that intense physical or emotional disturbances result when that drug is withdrawn or the behavior (such as gambling) is stopped.

When people are psychologically dependent, they have uncontrollable emotional cravings for a particular substance or activity. When deprived of it, they experience feelings of

THE BETTMANN ARCHIVE

This etching, entitled **There is Father!,** *makes plain the effect that alcoholism can have on a family.*

loss and uneasiness that border on the unbearable. These feelings are psychological withdrawal symptoms. A person typically develops a psychological dependence on an addictive activity as opposed to a psychoactive substance.

For example, there are compulsive gamblers who are as psychologically dependent as any heroin addict is physically dependent. Many gamblers find it impossible to give gambling up, even when it is leading them to personal, professional, and financial ruin. An organization called Gamblers Anonymous has been established to help these people, and it works exactly the same way Alcoholics Anonymous does.

The common behavior of shopping, when it becomes compulsive, can set up a psychological dependency in some people that makes shopping an irresistible activity even when they are spending themselves into severe financial distress.

Television viewing is a common, often intense psychological addiction. One study found that regular TV watchers, when deprived of their sets, felt a sense of loss comparable to that caused by a death in the family.

On the other hand, physical withdrawal symptoms occur when people are deprived of a psychoactive drug on which they have become dependent. Although physical and psychological withdrawal symptoms resemble each other in many respects, physical withdrawal symptoms are usually far more dire than psychological withdrawal symptoms. Physical withdrawal can involve nausea, vomiting, excessive perspiration, altered heartbeat and blood pressure, and bodily tremors (shakes). Sometimes these physical symptoms are severe, and they can be life-threatening.

Scientists believe that physical withdrawal symptoms from psychoactive drugs are related to the defenses the body throws up against these foreign substances in the first place. That is, the same "balancing" processes the body develops in an effort to counteract the effects of a drug, leading to a tolerance of that drug, continue to operate for some time after the drug is withdrawn. One reason why scientists believe that the same mechanisms underlying the cycles of tolerance and dependence are also responsible for withdrawal symptoms is that these symptoms are sometimes exactly the opposite of the effects of the drug itself. For example, in the case of depressants, the person undergoing withdrawal is often stimulated, suffering such symptoms as acute restlessness, insomnia, emotional outbursts, and shakiness.

The response of the body to alcohol is a good illustration of the ways in which a psychoactive drug promotes one reaction in the body while its withdrawal tends to result in the opposite reaction. Alcohol depresses many physical processes, causing slurred speech, staggering, and mental dullness. (Initially, of course, alcohol can promote such behaviors as talkativeness, sociability, and lowering of inhibitions, but these "positive" reactions quickly give way to the chemically depressing effects of the drug.) On the other hand, the withdrawal of alcohol tends to have a physiologically stimulating effect and can lead to tension, sleep disorders, extreme anxiety, and bodily tremors. These withdrawal symptoms occur when a heavy drinker is suddenly cut off from alcohol.

What Is Personality?

We often hear that a certain person does or does not have a "good" personality or that one person has "more" personality than another. When used in this everyday sense, the term

24

Table 1

Ancient Greek Theory of Body Humors	
PREDOMINANT HUMOR	CORRESPONDING PERSONALITY TYPE
Blood	Sanguine (optimistic)
Black bile	Melancholy (sad, depressed)
Yellow bile	Irascible (easily angered)
Phlegm	Phlegmatic (unemotional, quiet, serene)

personality refers to a person's skills in relating to other people. However, social skill is just one of many personality characteristics.

Psychologists are concerned with the nature of "personality" in its entirety. To them, the term *personality* has a technical meaning that is quite different from its common one. They use it to include an individual's entire range of personal characteristics. These include both desirable and undesirable qualities, and psychologists do not attempt to place value judgments on them.

How Do Psychologists View Personality?

Psychologists need to have a plan for thinking about personality and organizing the information they gather. Two common methods for making such a plan are the type approach and the trait approach.

The *type approach* involves placing people in personality categories. It has its origins in antiquity, having first been used by the ancient Greeks. Just as the Greeks believed that everything in physical nature was composed of four elements—earth, air, fire, and water—they believed that people's bodies were composed of four fluids, or humors, which they labeled blood, black bile, yellow bile, and phlegm. Personality was thought to be determined by the relative amount of each humor that was present in the body. The personality type that was supposed to correspond to each is shown in Table 1.

Although the Greeks' effort to categorize personality was a remarkably sophisticated undertaking for its time, we know today that their efforts were misguided. There is no validity to the theory of body humors.

A more recent type approach was developed by William Sheldon in the 1940s. He suggested that there is a relationship between body build and personality. Thus, his theory is called a body-type theory. Sheldon proposed that there are three basic body types—ectomorph, mesomorph, and endomorph. The descriptions of these body types are shown in Table 2.

Corresponding to each body type is a personality type. The names and descriptions of these three personality types are also shown in Table 2.

Although there are people who actually fit into Sheldon's categories, there are so many exceptions to his theory—or any body-type theory—that it has not gained wide accep-

Pablo Picasso's abstract sculptures **Les Baigneurs.** *The short, round-faced, and seemingly cheerful figure in the right foreground and the tall, somewhat aloof figure at the far left would aptly illustrate William Sheldon's body-type theory of personality.*

Table 2

Sheldon's Body-Type Theory			
BODY TYPE	DESCRIPTION	CORRESPONDING PERSONALITY TYPE	DESCRIPTION
Ectomorph	Tall and thin	Cerebrontonia	Shy and reserved, intellectual
Mesomorph	Large muscles and bones, athletic build	Somatontonia	Outgoing, interested in sports and other bodily and outdoor activities
Endomorph	Short and fat	Viscerotonia	Jolly, good-natured, outgoing

tance among medical professionals. No relationship between body build and personality has ever been scientifically demonstrated. Moreover, even if such a relationship were to be established, it would be impossible to explain. Body-type theories imply that certain body types give rise to corresponding personalities. However, there would be no way to rule out the possibility that, on the contrary, certain personality traits determine body type.

Another modern type approach for understanding personality was developed by the eminent Swiss psychiatrist Carl Jung in the early 20th century. Jung claimed that personality could be classified into two different types which he subdivided into *functions* and *attitudes*. According to the Jungian theory, functions were ways of judging and dealing with all of life's experiences. Jung claimed that personality was governed by four such functions—cognition (thinking), emotion (feeling), sensation, and intuition. The attitudes were introversion and extroversion, and, according to Jung, each function could be introverted or extroverted. Jung believed that the four functions were all available to each of us, but that, for whatever reason, one of them would come to dominate and determine the ways in which a particular person usually or typically behaves.

Jung and all others who have proposed type theories of personality as a way of understanding human nature and behavior allow that no one person could possibly be pigeonholed into one rigidly defined category or another. However, psychologists who believe in type theories do maintain that this approach allows them to come as close as possible to defining what any individual is "really" like. But the problem with all type theories is that there is a stubborn complexity and variety in human nature which ultimately resists such inflexible scientific categorization.

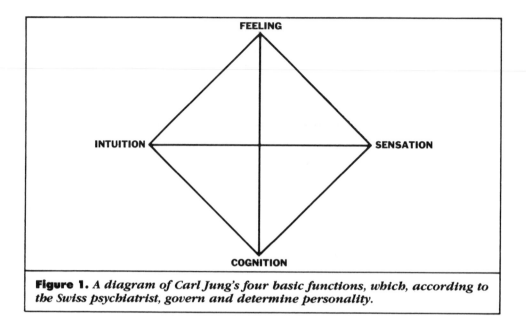

Figure 1. *A diagram of Carl Jung's four basic functions, which, according to the Swiss psychiatrist, govern and determine personality.*

Recognizing the limitations of type theories as a means of labeling an individual's primary approach to life, certain psychologists working in the field of personality theory developed what are called *trait theories*. Needless to say, there are a countless number of personality traits. In fact, when psychologist Gordon Allport, a leading advocate of the trait theory, set out to develop his system, one of the first things he did was to look through an unabridged dictionary for all the adjectives that could be used to describe personality. His list included 16,000 terms!

Working to systematize his long list, Allport incorporated terms that had similar meanings—such as *happy, glad, cheerful,* and *optimistic.* He then used a sophisticated statistical technique called "factor analysis" to group these synonyms. The terms clustered together were called a "factor." Each factor was given a name that best represented all of the terms included in that factor. Allport concluded that personality can be completely described by 16 factors. He also developed a personality test called the Sixteen Personality-Factor Questionnaire to measure these factors.

Similar to trait theories is another approach to personality that views it in terms of different categories of psychopathology (psychological disturbance). This method differs from the trait approaches only in that it describes personality in terms of abnormalities and disturbances, rather than in terms of traits which encompass all kinds of behaviors. There are many kinds of psychopathology that can be included, such as depression, anxiety, and psychosomatic disorders. When psychologists evaluate personality according to this method, the subject of the evaluation is given a score in each of several categories. Someone might score high on one or more of the categories or score high on none of them. Since psychopathological traits are exaggerated forms of "normal" personality characteristics, the personalities of people who are not psychologically disturbed can also be described using this method.

A modern theory of personality was offered by Swiss psychiatrist Carl Jung (1875–1961), who placed people into categories, ranging from extremely shy to extremely gregarious. Later, Harvard psychologist Gordon Allport proposed 16 "factors" according to which personality could be comprehensively analyzed.

Still another set of terms that psychologists have developed to discuss personality are called situation-specific personality characteristics. This approach begins with the assumption that a person's environment or any particular situation in which the person happens to be will most strongly determine his or her behavior in that environment or situation. For example, a person might be quiet in one situation or with certain people but talkative and outgoing under other circumstances and with different company. The fact that people generally have fairly consistent patterns of behavior allows psychologists to categorize personality according to the kinds of behavior most often or typically exhibited.

How Do Psychologists Measure Personality?

Psychologists have developed tests to measure personality characteristics. A number of these tests have been used with substance abusers. These have been helpful in enhancing our understanding of why certain individuals abuse alcohol and other drugs, and in describing the ways in which addicts differ from nonaddicts.

Broadly speaking, psychological tests are either projective or objective. The essential characteristic of all *projective tests* is that they make use of ambiguous stimuli—that is, those that are open to many interpretations. These stimuli are presented to subjects taking the test, and they tell what the stimuli mean to them. Since the stimuli have no special meaning, any meaning that the subjects give to the stimuli must come from within themselves. Hence, people taking this kind of test "project" their own personality—their needs, feelings, and motives—onto the stimuli.

Although all projective tests use ambiguous stimuli, the degree to which the stimuli are ambiguous does vary widely from test to test. The most ambiguous stimuli are found in the Rorschach test. This test was constructed in the early 20th century by Swiss psychiatrist Hermann Rorschach, who devised it by dropping ink on pieces of paper and then creasing the paper in the center in order to make the inkblot symmetrical. He transposed these inkblots onto 10 standardized cards. People taking the Rorschach test are handed the cards one by one and are asked to say what the inkblot looks like to them or what it reminds them of and why. Experience

Moods, as interpreted by a French artist, take on a romantic intensity. There are two methods psychologists use in organizing ways to distinguish personalities. The type approach, first used by the ancient Greeks, involves placing people in personality categories. Trait theories, as advocated by Gordon Allport, emphasize personality characteristics.

with the test and well-established rules of interpretation allow the psychologist giving the test to learn a great deal about the subject's personality on the basis of how he or she responds to each inkblot.

A projective test that uses stimuli far less ambiguous than the inkblots in the Rorschach test is the thematic apperception test (TAT). The TAT uses a set of cards with scenes on them. Most people can clearly identify the objects or people pictured in the scenes. What is ambiguous about the scenes is what events are taking place. People taking the TAT are asked to invent a story about the scene on each card, describing what is taking place, the events leading up to it, and

THE BETTMANN ARCHIVE

A 19th-century engraving of a priest attending to a man suffering from terrifying hallucinations. In modern culture, psychiatrists and psychologists have become alternatives to clergymen as possible healers of sick souls.

what the outcome will be. In so doing, subjects unconsciously project themselves into the story they are creating. The subjects are thought to identify with one of the characters in the story, thereby unconsciously revealing their own motives, wishes, and personality characteristics.

While the people taking projective tests are often unaware that they are disclosing information about their own personality, in *objective tests* people are asked to describe their own personality traits directly. The first objective test (published in 1920) was the Woodworth Personal Data Sheet. It would be obvious to anyone taking this test or one like it what sorts of traits were being measured by each section of the test.

Objective personality tests are based on two assumptions: (1) that people know what their own personality characteristics are and (2) that they will answer questions about their personality accurately and truthfully. It is now obvious that these assumptions are not always valid. People frequently don't know themselves all that well and are often likely to provide inaccurate information. A person's self-image can be distorted for any number of reasons. This leaves people incapable of describing their own personalities objectively. In addition, there are many situations (such as applying for a job) in which someone might have very compelling reasons for being less than honest when asked for a self-evaluation.

A test that was created in part to correct the distorted and inconclusive findings associated with certain other objective tests is the Minnesota Multiphasic Personality Inventory (MMPI). This is the test that has been used most often to study addictive personality characteristics. Developed at the University of Minnesota, where it was first published in 1940, this test is called multiphasic because it measures and scores numerous aspects of personality. It is called a personality inventory because people who are taking the test make an "inventory" (take stock) of their own personality by indicating whether each of 566 statements is true or false for them. While the methods used to score the MMPI are quite complicated and involved, Table 3 provides a general outline of the kinds of categories and descriptions that the test uses to measure and evaluate personality.

The MMPI has a much wider application than the diagnosis of abnormal behavior. It is also used to study per-

Table 3

Description of Clinical Scales from MMPI

Hypochondriasis (Hs)
People who score high on this scale tend to have imaginary or exaggerated physical complaints. In reality, their psychological problems are being expressed in the form of bodily complaints.

Depression (D)
People who score high on the depression scale feel sad and dejected. They are pessimistic about the future, and they do not derive normal enjoyment from life.

Hysteria (Hy)
High scores on this scale are achieved by people who have real physical problems, but the problems have psychological rather than organic causes. The physical symptoms develop as an inappropriate way of trying to solve the psychological conflicts.

Psychopathic Deviate (Pd)
High scores on the Pd scale are obtained by people who do not respect the traditional customs and values of society. Although they have good social skills, they have difficulty forming intimate, enduring relationships with other people. They are also unable to profit from their mistakes.

Masculinity-Femininity (Mf)
This scale is keyed in opposite directions for males and females. Males who score high on the scale tend to have intellectual, cultural, or artistic interest, and shun aggressive and typically masculine activities. Females who score low on the scale tend to have these same interest and activity patterns.

Paranoia (Pa)
A high score on the Pa scale indicates people who have distorted views of reality. They may be suspicious of the motives of other people, believing themselves to be the victims of persecution, or they may have an unrealistically high regard for themselves, believing themselves to be exalted people.

Psychasthenia (Pt)
People who score high on this scale feel anxious and insecure, and they worry a great deal. They may have obsessive thoughts or carry out compulsive acts in an attempt to cope with their anxieties.

Schizophrenia (Sc)
High scores on the Sc scale are generally obtained by people who have retreated into a world of unreality. Their thought processes are distorted, and their emotional reactions may be inappropriate.

Hypomania (Ma)
Hypomanic people are very energetic, and they are unable to concentrate on one topic for very long. They have unrealistic plans and schemes.

Social Introversion (Si)
Social introverts are people who either feel uncomfortable socializing with other people or lack the social skills required to do so. To other people, they seem withdrawn and aloof.

sonality in general. For instance, people with a very high score on the paranoia scale would be seen as having delusions (fixed beliefs which have no basis in reality.) On the other hand, people with a mild elevation on the paranoia scale may simply be highly sensitive to the feelings and desires of others. However self-destructive or generally inappropriate the behavior of those with addictive personalities may be, such people tend not to achieve exaggerated scores on most of the personality scales from the MMPI.

With the above in mind we can now go on to look at the specifics of drug abuse and the kinds of people who are most vulnerable to addiction.

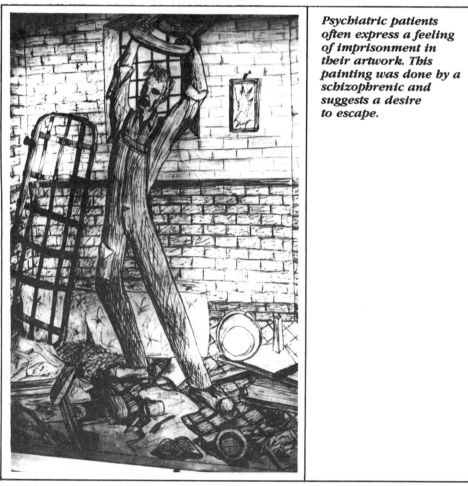

Psychiatric patients often express a feeling of imprisonment in their artwork. This painting was done by a schizophrenic and suggests a desire to escape.

Sigmund Freud (1856–1939), founder of psychoanalysis. Freud's theories about the development of personality and his techniques for treating disturbed persons have enhanced our understanding of all addictive behaviors.

CHAPTER 2

HISTORICAL OVERVIEW OF PERSONALITY AND ADDICTIVE BEHAVIOR

*S*tarting in the 1970s, the problems associated with drug abuse and addiction began to receive an ever-increasing amount of attention. However, the phenomenon of addiction itself is by no means recent. Addictions have been a major public health problem in the United States for at least a hundred years.

Drug addiction seems to have taken on major proportions in American society during and just after the Civil War. One factor that gave rise to addictive behavior at this time was the unwise use of the drug morphine (morphine is the pure narcotic that is derived from the opium poppy plant, and it is many times as potent as opium itself). Scientists had learned to extract pure morphine from the poppy plant in the early 1800s, and morphine became very widely used for medicinal purposes during the Civil War. Its use was facilitated by the invention of the hypodermic syringe, which allowed morphine to be injected directly into the bloodstream, producing a potent and immediate effect.

There are several legitimate uses for morphine. First and foremost, morphine is a very effective painkiller, with obvious applications for wounded or dying soldiers during a war. Morphine, which is constipating, is also a good treatment for dysentery—a severe form of diarrhea that was widespread during the Civil War.

Since it was not known initially that morphine is addicting, physicians at first had no reservations about giving it to their patients, often indiscriminately. Morphine addiction among Civil War soldiers became so common that it was referred to as the "soldier's disease" and the "army's disease."

The widespread use of patent medicines in the mid-1800s also served to make addiction a large-scale problem. These "medicines" did not really cure the underlying physical illnesses. However, since they contained potent psychoactive drugs such as heroin, morphine, cocaine, and THC (from the marijuana plant), these concoctions did have powerful psychological effects, giving people the impression that the medicine was curing them. Needless to say, these drugs merely acted on the symptoms of the illnesses.

Patent medicines could be purchased legally without a physician's prescription. Thus, they were distributed by traveling salespeople, sold in local stores, and could be ordered from catalogs. Manufacturers made extraordinary claims for these potions—all of them inaccurate and some of them downright false. Not until the Pure Food and Drug Act was passed in 1906, firmly regulating the use and distribution of these potent medicines, was there any legal control over them.

Alcoholism and Other Drug Addictions

Until recently, our understanding of addictive behavior has been both unsophisticated and moralistic. Early laws to regulate the flow of narcotics, such as the Pure Food and Drug Act and the Harrison Narcotics Act of 1914, were based largely on the assumption that controlling drug addiction was simply a matter of making the sale and use of narcotics illegal except under tightly regulated conditions. Similar thinking, which held that drugs and alcohol were in themselves somehow "evil" or "demonic," lay behind the 18th Amendment to the U.S. Constitution. The amendment sought to eliminate the consumption of alcohol entirely by making its production and sale illegal. It took effect in 1920 and began what was known as Prohibition.

Contrary to popular opinion, the consumption of alcohol did go down significantly during Prohibition, but the 18th

Amendment proved essentially unenforceable and it was repealed in 1933. There is always a direct connection between the general availability of any drug and the amount that gets consumed. However, society has learned the hard way that it cannot outlaw addiction simply by making drugs illegal or even by carefully regulating their legal use. A vast criminal empire dedicated exclusively to the illegal sale and distribution of narcotics and other psychoactive drugs testifies to this fact.

Equally unhelpful in treating and curing addictive behavior was the early view that the afflicted were suffering from moral weakness or character disorders. While drug and alcohol abuse lead in many cases to unacceptable behavior, enlightened opinion today holds that people do not become addicts because they are "sinful" or "bad" to begin with and that overcoming addiction is not a simple matter of moral fortitude or willpower.

WIDE WORLD PICTURES

A girl weeds an opium field in the "Golden Triangle" of Southeast Asia. Despite laws that control opium's use, illicit trafficking persists.

A more scientifically sound view of addiction is that it is a disease. The disease concept was first introduced in 1812 by the physician Benjamin Rush, who proposed that hospitals be established especially for the treatment of alcoholics. Other 19th-century physicians attempted to promote the disease concept, and a new professional journal, the *Journal of Inebriety*, was established especially for this purpose. However, throughout the 19th and early 20th centuries, the disease concept of alcoholism was not widely accepted.

It was not until the failure of attempts to prohibit addictive drugs in society that people began seriously to consider explanations of addictive behavior other than the "moral weakness" and "demonic drug" explanations. Following the repeal of Prohibition, the disease concept, as well as some psychologically oriented explanations of addiction began to receive serious attention.

Alcoholism Following Prohibition

By the end of the Prohibition era, American society realized how misguided it had been to attempt to eliminate alcohol problems by prohibiting alcohol entirely. Although fewer

UPI/BETTMANN ARCHIVE

Celebrating the end of Prohibition, a large, happy crowd at the St. Moritz Hotel grill in New York City drinks an alcoholic toast at one minute after midnight on April 7, 1933. Although fewer people consumed alcoholic beverages during Prohibition, the number of drinkers with alcohol-related problems may have actually increased.

people drank during the 13 years of Prohibition, there is some evidence that the number of people who developed problems with alcohol actually increased. Alcohol continued to be available, although it could not be obtained legally. Bootleg operations flourished. Once it became apparent that the Prohibition approach was totally ineffective, the "demon alcohol" explanation of abuse was pretty much laid to rest. The time was ripe for more sophisticated and useful theories of alcohol abuse.

Founded in 1935, Alcoholics Anonymous (AA) has played a crucial role in reviving the disease concept of alcoholism. A self-help organization, AA was formed to enable and encourage alcoholics to help each other overcome their addiction. The primary philosophy of AA is that alcoholism is a disease of both the mind and the body—not a moral weakness—and that alcoholics must abstain completely from alcohol in order to deal with their disease.

According to AA's interpretation of the disease concept, whenever alcoholics ingest even the most moderate amounts of alcohol, their bodies set up an allergic reaction to it, which, somewhat paradoxically, drives them to increase their consumption. Thus, according to AA, for alcoholics there is no

Benjamin Rush (left) proposed that hospitals be established especially for the treatment of alcoholics. At right is a drawing of his "tranquilizing" chair, which he used to restrain unmanageable patients.

such thing as drinking "in moderation." Unless they abstain completely, their old drinking patterns will sooner or later re-establish themselves, no matter how long they may have managed to abstain from alcohol or control their intake of it. AA holds that an alcoholic's disease is an integral part of his or her personality and that the alcoholic must undergo a fundamental personality change in order to recover from that disease.

Although the theories of Alcoholics Anonymous have gained increasing acceptance in the medical community and among most counselors and therapists who deal with alcoholism, there are also other legitimate theories about alcoholism that attempt to define and treat the condition.

Psychiatrists—doctors who specialize in the treatment of mental disorders—first turned their attention to the problems of alcoholism at about the time Prohibition was repealed in 1933. As practiced by psychiatrists, psychoanalysis is both a theory about how psychological disturbances and personality in general develop and a technique for treating these disturbances. According to psychoanalytic theory, psychological disturbances can be traced to events that occurred during early childhood. This theory emphasizes the importance of early childhood experiences in personality formation and the importance of delving into the past in order to treat a person with psychological problems.

THE BETTMANN ARCHIVE

Women of the Prohibition period gather at a "speakeasy" bar. It is estimated that some 17 million Americans are afflicted with alcoholism. Although this addiction is more prevalent among men than women, the proportion of female alcoholics is increasing.

Let us first consider some of the general principles of psychoanalytic theory and then see how these principles can be applied to an understanding of alcoholism. Psychoanalysts believe that a person's basic personality structure is formed during the first six years of life. They see young children as passing through three successive stages of development during this time—the oral, anal, and genital stages.

The oral stage covers the first year of life. During this time, young children find pleasure primarily through activities involving their mouths—such as cooing, biting, chewing, sucking, and eating. At this age, children are entirely dependent on their parents for the satisfaction of all their bodily and psychological needs, especially those needs that center on eating. The relationship between parents and children is delicate at this time. For instance, parents may frustrate their children and not allow them enough "oral" stimulation, or the parents may give their children excessive oral stimulation by constantly pampering and indulging them. In either

"Duckboard" Butler, a public-safety director during Prohibition, happily destroys a keg of beer, draining its contents into the Schuylkill River in Philadelphia.

case, the children may grow up to have oral personality characteristics, spending much of their time in the oral activities that they were so fond of or were deprived of enjoying during this stage. Examples of adult oral personality characteristics include smoking, excessive eating or drinking (including drinking alcohol), and symbolic oral gestures such as being "biting" or sarcastic toward other people.

During the second and third years of life, according to psychoanalytic theory, young children are in the anal stage of development. At this time, the life of the child is centered on the elimination of waste products from the body. Toilet training takes place during this stage. If the toilet training proceeds smoothly, the child's chances of being well adjusted in adult life are enhanced. On the other hand, if toilet training becomes a battleground between parents and child, the child is apt to develop emotional conflicts and personality problems that could last a lifetime. Psychoanalysts maintain that adult hostility, obsessive attention to detail, and compulsive neatness are often the result of tension-ridden toilet-training experiences.

AP/WIDE WORLD PHOTOS

The artwork of disturbed children can help in the diagnosis of their mental distress. At left, Grace says goodbye to her horse and walks to her grave. Hank's drawing (right) of knives pointed at a naked woman expresses both a fear of mutilation and the desire to retaliate.

At about age four, children enter the genital stage of development. This stage has two distinguishing characteristics: (1) Children become highly aware of and focused on their genitals, and (2) parent-child relationships at this stage are crucial to the development of future personality characteristics. At this stage, little boys enter what Sigmund Freud labeled the Oedipal period, meaning that their love for their mothers becomes intense and possessive, and they have a corresponding fear, jealousy, and resentment toward their fathers. (Freud invented the term *Oedipus complex* to describe these feelings after Oedipus, the king of Thebes in ancient Greek mythology who unknowingly killed his father and married his mother.) Eventually, according to Freud, most boys resolve their Oedipal feelings and come to identify with their fathers. That is, they think of themselves as being like their fathers and having the same masculine attributes.

The reverse situation occurs with young girls at this stage. Girls come to resent their mothers and develop an emotional attachment to their fathers. Freud named these intense feelings of a little girl for her father the *Electra com-*

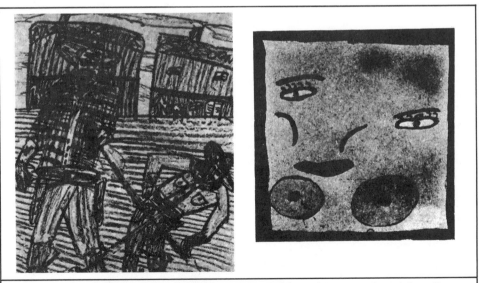

Two more pictures by mentally unstable children: Tom used rigid and angular lines to show a man (left) "engulfed in thoughts of hate." At right, Mary illustrates her own infantile conception of her mother; mouth and breasts dominate the picture.

plex, again borrowing from Greek mythology. (Electra was strongly attached to her father and plotted the murder of her mother.) Freud held that most girls resolve these feelings the same way boys do—that is, by identifying with and modeling themselves after the parents of the same sex.

According to psychoanalytic theory, if for some reason a child is severely frustrated at any one of these three stages, he or she will remain psychologically fixated (trapped) at that stage rather than proceeding to the next stage. The fixation will be reflected in adult personality disorders.

Psychoanalysts believe that alcoholics tend to be individuals who were somehow frustrated at the oral stage. The oral fixation is inferred from alcoholics' over-dependence on other people, their immaturity, and their inability to withstand frustration and postpone immediate pleasure in the interest of achieving long-range goals.

Among male alcoholics the situation is more complicated than among female alcoholics, because at the same time that males are often orally fixated and have a strong need to be dependent on other people, they have an equally strong

A 19th-century woodcut of a smoker. According to Freudian theory, adults fixated at the oral stage of development—which comprises the first year of life and is primarily concerned with biting, sucking, and eating—are likely to engage habitually in oral activities such as smoking, drinking, or excessive eating.

need to be independent, masculine, and aggressive. Thus, male alcoholics have strong conflicts about their opposing needs. Drinking alcohol helps them relieve the conflict and allows them to satisfy both needs at the same time. Heavy drinking is clearly a masculine activity, but it provides oral stimulation as well. Moreover, it is socially acceptable for the intoxicated male to be dependent on other people, allowing them to take care of him.

Although psychoanalysts have attempted to treat alcoholics, it is generally acknowledged that psychoanalysis—a form of long-term "talk therapy" in which a patient attempts to uncover troubling and forgotten events from early childhood and hence render them less disturbing—is not particularly effective in the treatment of addictive or compulsive behavior. Nevertheless, psychoanalytic theories of personality in general have contributed a great deal to an enlightened and humane view of addictive behavior. However much Freud's ideas may have been modified or even discredited over the years, his views on the connection between early experience and personality development helped to pave the way for an approach to addictive behavior that looked for its origins in personality. However much prejudice may linger in society's attitudes towards alcoholics and other drug abusers, they can no longer be dismissed by knowledgeable people as morally deficient or as victims of a strictly physical disease. Nor, as was the case with Prohibitionists, can we any longer simply label psychoactive substances inherently "evil" and attempt to stop their use by banning them.

While addictive behavior is not restricted to the compulsive use of psychoactive substances, scientists have learned much more about the connections between personality and drug abuse than they have about the link between personality and compulsive gambling, for instance. Moreover, at this point theoretical knowledge about the link between personality and alcoholism is much more advanced than knowledge about the connections between personality and addiction to other psychoactive drugs. Thus, as we continue our investigation of the addictive personality, we will focus primarily on the problems of alcohol use and misuse. Whenever possible, we will also compare what is known about personality and alcohol with what is known about personality and other psychoactive drugs.

The Addictive Personality

The concept of an addictive personality arose as a result of changing views on the causes of alcoholism. Psychoanalysis promoted personality as the major alternative to the "moral weakness" and "demonic drug" explanations of alcoholism. In fact, during the years following the end of Prohibition, the idea of an "alcoholic personality" was widely accepted among psychoanalysts. The alcoholic personality was presumed to be unique to alcoholics, and it was regarded as the sole cause of alcohol abuse. The alcoholic personality was also consistent with the disease concept of alcoholism.

Psychologists now recognize that the addictive personality—alcoholic or otherwise—is an overly simplistic concept, perhaps as misguided as the other single-cause explanations of alcoholism. Alcoholism is a complex phenomenon, and many factors in addition to personality con-

A man nurses a drink at a cafe. Many people begin to abuse drugs such as alcohol to alleviate anxiety, tension, or depression.

tribute to its development. Among these are biological factors (inherited biochemical reactions to psychoactive drugs), environmental factors (such as peer pressure), sociocultural factors that influence a person to drink heavily or moderately, and psychological factors other than personality (such as people's expectations about the effects that drugs will have on them). Any given individual might be affected to varying degrees by any or all of these contributing causes of alcoholism.

Biological factors may make a person prone to alcoholism primarily because of the body's inherited biochemical reactivity to alcohol. Some people have a strong positive reaction to alcohol and can often drink large quantities of it with few negative side effects. Such people feel that alcohol has always enhanced their self-image and heightened life's pleasures. Conversely, there are some people who have almost no physical tolerance for alcohol. Even the most moderate amounts of it result in severe physical distress, such as flushed skin, nausea, and headache. These people have a built-in biological protection against becoming alcoholics. This reaction to alcohol is common among Orientals, who, as a result, have a relatively low rate of alcoholism.

Environmental factors strongly influence people's drinking decisions and help to determine whether or not they develop drinking problems. These factors have to do with the extent to which drinking is promoted or discouraged in a person's immediate environment. Specific examples of such environmental factors include the availability of alcohol, advertising, and other promotion of alcoholic beverages as well as the extent to which other people—especially one's peers—drink and encourage others to do likewise.

Sociocultural factors are closely related to environmental factors and have to do with the drinking customs of the culture in which a person lives. Some cultures have very high rates of alcoholism, and it is very likely that a person growing up in such a culture will develop problems with alcohol. Other cultures have very low rates of alcoholism, and it is relatively unlikely that a person growing up in such a culture will develop a drinking problem. For example, alcohol abuse is common in Ireland and in France. Among Irish males, heavy drinking ("drinking like a man") is considered very *macho*. Among the French, it is customary to drink wine on a daily basis—with meals, between meals, and at work. As a consequence of this heavy social drinking, people in France tend to develop a form of alcoholism called *delta alcoholism*. The distinguishing characteristic of delta alcoholism is the inability to abstain from alcohol. Although people with this type of alcohol problem generally do not drink large quantities on a single occasion and hence tend not to become intoxicated, they usually cannot totally abstain from alcohol for even brief periods of time without suffering from withdrawal symptoms. It's as if they have to have low levels of alcohol in their bloodstream practically all the time.

On the other hand, Italian and Jewish cultures have relatively low rates of alcoholism. In both of these cultures, children are taught how to drink alcohol from an early age. Parents may give their children a glass of wine to drink at mealtime or to celebrate a religious observance or some festive occasion, but drinking heavily and drunkenness are strictly forbidden. The culture socially ostracizes any person who drinks to excess. As a consequence of these standards, children in these cultures tend to grow up knowing how to drink alcohol sensibly and in moderation.

People's expectations about drinking are an example of the psychological factors that play a strong role in the development of drinking habits, regardless of personality. Detailed and complex experiments have demonstrated that the effect a person expects to get from drinking and the actual pharmacological effect of alcohol do not always coincide. Moreover, the expected effect of alcohol often affects behavior more than the pharmacological action of alcohol.

The value of such findings lies in the fact that they allow the pharmacological and expected effects of alcohol to be separated. It has been demonstrated under experimental conditions that if people expect to receive alcohol and do receive it, they are affected both by its chemical properties and by their own expectations. By the same token, if people are told they are being given a nonalcoholic beverage and are given a nonalcoholic beverage, they experience no effects. On the other hand, someone who expects to receive alcohol and gets a nonalcoholic drink instead experiences only the expected effects. People who expect to receive a nonalcoholic drink and are given alcohol experience only the pharmacological effects of the alcohol.

Using studies based on such experiments, researchers have come to the conclusion that people who bring intense expectations—either positive or negative—to drinking are more likely to develop problems with alcohol than those who do not.

To be sure, there are many forces which singly or in combination can lead to addictive behavior. But where does personality fit into the profile of an addict, and what can psychologists learn about addiction by focusing on personality? Can tendencies to addiction be predicted on the basis of certain personality traits that actually precede the addictive behavior? Are the personalities of addicts specifically different from those of nonaddicts, and if so, in what ways? Finally, what effects do addictive substances have on personality, and how do such substances alter personality over time?

We will now address these questions and look at the conclusions that modern psychologists have reached in their efforts to understand the relationship between personality and addiction.

Environmental factors influence the decisions people make about drinking. Here, a sign in a Paris subway station asks "Are you quite sure you're sober?" and the slogan at right reads "Health, Sobriety."

An etching entitled Crazed by Opium. *The narcotic opium, which is found in such highly addictive drugs as morphine and heroin, quickly induces tolerance in people who take it, meaning that higher dosages of the drug are needed in order to achieve the original effects.*

CHAPTER 3

PRE-ADDICTIVE PERSONALITY CHARACTERISTICS

Are people who develop problems with alcohol and other drugs somehow different from other people even before their drug problems begin? This is a very important question. For example, there are obvious advantages in being able to determine who might be likely to develop alcohol problems before the patterns of addiction are established. Such people could be cautioned to shy away from alcohol, warned that they have a unique vulnerability, and assured that whatever the immediate short-term pleasures of alcohol might be its long-term consequences could be disastrous.

Methods of Study

However, at the present time there is no way to know in advance who will develop problems with alcohol. Researchers who are interested in locating pre-addictive personality traits must either work backwards once addiction has set in or study large groups over many years, beginning before the onset of any addiction problems, pinpointing addiction once it sets in, and then retracing the path the addicts have taken for clues in their personalities that may have made them destined for addiction.

Given all the pitfalls in identifying pre-addictive personality traits the longitudinal method of study would be the most accurate and objective way to go about it. Using the longitudinal method, one would choose a large group of people to be studied from a time early in their lives until a time much later in their lives, when some of the people had developed alcohol problems. The subjects in the study would be given a comprehensive personality test both at the beginning of the study and at frequent intervals thereafter in order to monitor changes in their personality across time. The subjects' use of any psychoactive drugs would also need to be carefully monitored. Eventually, once addiction had set in, one could analyze all the collected data with an eye to determining in which ways, if any, addicts had differed from nonaddicts all along.

Longitudinal studies are costly and difficult to undertake, however. And since statistics show that only a small percentage of people eventually become addicts, personality tests would have to be given to a large group of people early in their lives and repeated regularly until some of them eventually became addicted. One more specific approach would be to do a longitudinal study on the sons of alcoholics, who, statistics show, are about four times as likely to become alcoholics as other people. But it might take 20 years to come to any valid conclusions using the longitudinal approach—to say nothing of the enormous cost of such a study.

An alternative to a longitudinal study would be to question alcoholics about their pre-alcoholic personality charac-

teristics. One could also question their families and friends. But this method is obviously vulnerable to all the subjectivity and distortion that tend to color people's perceptions and understanding of each other and themselves.

A more objective method is to search for earlier records kept on alcoholics prior to the onset of drinking problems. Often they provide information about the pre-alcoholic personalities of the addicts. Because this method involves studying historical records, it is referred to as the archival method. The major drawback of this method is that the data have usually been quite limited. Nevertheless, some interesting observations about pre-alcoholics' personality characteristics have been gathered using archival studies.

Pre-alcoholic Personality Characteristics

Because of the difficulties involved, no longitudinal studies that follow alcoholics during the full development of their alcohol problems have been completed. However, such studies are currently in progress.

A number of other studies have been completed that have followed subjects for relatively brief periods. These studies have followed adolescents, typically prior to the time when they began drinking until the time when they began to develop drinking problems. The results of these studies

A series of French postcards entitled Ten Nights in a Barroom *depicts the decline of a man because of his addiction to alcohol. Although the pictures in this collection are highly melodramatic, alcoholism is a serious problem that can, if left untreated, be debilitating and sometimes fatal.*

consistently point to a common conclusion: even before adolescents develop problems with alcohol, their personality characteristics are different from those of adolescents who do not later develop problems with alcohol. Namely, they are independent, rebellious, and do not uphold the traditional values of society. (In contrast to the personality characteristics of future problem drinkers, there are indications that adolescents who develop problems with harder illegal drugs are psychologically disturbed. Such adolescents have been found to suffer from anxiety, depression, low self-esteem, and other manifestations of maladjustment.)

One interesting archival study that was carried out in Minnesota made use of the Minnesota Multiphasic Personality Inventory. Between the years 1947 and 1961, the MMPI was administered to all incoming freshmen at the University of Minnesota. The results were kept on file at the University's Student Counseling Bureau in case a student needed to go to the bureau for personal counseling. Eventually, some people who were students during these years became alcoholics and sought help for their problem at a treatment center.

Reseachers at two treatment centers in Minnesota searched their files to identify alcoholic patients who had previously been students at the university. Thirty-two such

Samuel Taylor Coleridge, the noted British poet and critic, was an opium addict for many years. Alcoholism and drug abuse often occur among artistic people, many of whom are rebellious, impulsive, and easily bored.

THE BETTMANN ARCHIVE

patients were identified. To determine if the 32 patients had distinctive personality characteristics before they became alcoholics, the researchers selected a random sample of their former classmates, with whom the alcoholics could be compared.

The comparison of the University of Minnesota MMPI of these two groups indicated that overall the two personality profiles were similar. The profiles of the pre-alcoholics and their classmates represented "normal" profiles, indicating no maladjustment or psychological distress. On the other hand, closer inspection of the individual scores indicated that in three areas the pre-alcoholics scored higher than their classmates. These differences indicated that the pre-alcoholics were more independent, gregarious, and impulsive than their classmates, although not more maladjusted. Conversely, the MMPIs that the patients took when they entered the treatment program reflected significant psychological disturbances.

Several other archival studies have been carried out that support the conclusion of the Minnesota study—namely, that before people develop drinking problems they are different from other people in that they are more nonconformist, independent, undercontrolled, and impulsive.

Self-portrait *(1934) by Käthe Kollwitz, German graphic artist and sculptor. Kollwitz's illustrations often depict women suffering from the abuses of hunger and alcoholism. Recent findings indicate that while low self-esteem is common among all problem drinkers, these feelings are especially intense among women alcoholics.*

CHAPTER 4

ALCOHOLIC PERSONALITY CHARACTERISTICS

*U*nlike the relative scarcity of information on the personality characteristics of pre-alcoholics, there is a wealth of information on the personality characteristics of alcoholics. In this chapter we will review the methods for studying alcoholic personality characteristics and the evidence that has been gathered by these methods.

Methods of Study

Most of the information about personality characteristics of alcoholics has been gathered from alcoholics undergoing treatment. The groups studied are typically drawn from such institutions as mental health clinics, Veterans Administration medical centers, and state mental hospitals. The general procedure is to administer a personality test to the patients, report the results in the form of a group average for the test, and compare the results with those from other patients who are not substance abusers.

The difficulties with this method involve the fact that we cannot be certain whether the patients in treatment are representative of all substance abusers. Furthermore, the procedure of averaging the scores of all the patients has been questioned on the grounds that it may obscure important differences among the individual patients.

Because of these complications, researchers are tending more and more frequently to gather their data from sources other than patients in treatment. For instance, they attempt to gather data from people whose drinking problems are not severe enough for them to undergo formal treatment as well as from non-problem alcohol users to determine how patterns of consumption (that is, quantity and frequency of intake) might be related to personality characteristics.

Several other methods have been used to gather information about the personality characteristics of people who are already using or abusing addictive substances. These include studying people who are receiving individual treatment for their substance abuse from a psychologist or psychiatrist and people who may have developed problems with addictive substances but are not in treatment as substance abusers (such as college students) to see how the degree of use is related to personality.

The study of the substance abuser who is in individual treatment is referred to as the clinical case study method.

A study by David McClelland (center) on student drinking at Harvard suggested that heavy drinkers have a great need to exercise power.

With this method, the psychologist or psychiatrist who works with the individual patient writes a description of the client's personality, often including information from personality tests that have been administered to the client. The clinical case study method provides useful insights into how the client's substance abuse is related to his or her personality, but there is always some uncertainty about the extent to which information gathered from one substance abuser can be generalized to others.

Studying drug users who are not officially classified as substance abusers is particularly useful in the case of some drugs where there is no clear distinction between drug use and drug abuse. The caffeine in coffee is a good example of this. Although some people may drink large amounts of coffee on a daily basis and develop problems as a result, we have no clear guidelines for distinguishing caffeine users from caffeine abusers. With regard to other drugs, such as alcohol, it is often convenient to study relationships between alcohol use and personality among college students, but we must exercise caution in generalizing beyond the actual students tested.

Minnesota Multiphasic Personality Inventory

The most clear-cut evidence that alcoholics are unusually independent, nonconformist, and impulsive is provided by their performance on the Minnesota Multiphasic Personality Inventory, where they consistently register high scores on the scale called "psychopathic deviate." In fact, such scores constitute the most consistent finding from the extensive research on alcoholic personality characteristics. These results have held true during more than 40 years of research on tests administered to alcoholics from different walks of life.

The degree to which alcoholics score high in the psychopathic deviate scale indicates that the standards by which they conduct their lives are somewhat different from those of other people in our society. They are less likely to accept traditional social values and feel little remorse for not doing so. They are also people who tend to do things on the spur of the moment and are frustrated when they cannot immediately get what they want. Upon making mistakes, they are often unable to change their behavior so as to avoid repeating the mistake.

Data from the MMPI also provide information about alcoholics' relationships with other people. They tend to socialize well and generally have little difficulty thinking of appropriate things to say when meeting a person for the first time.

However, in spite of their sociability alcoholics often experience difficulty in their interpersonal relationships, particularly in the areas of intimacy and commitment. Because of this, alcoholics are frequently frustrated in their personal lives and feel that other people do not understand them.

Alcoholics are especially prone to experiencing these difficulties with members of their own family. They have frequent and intense disagreements with other family members and have a generally unpleasant home life. Constant difficulties with other people tend to result in bitterness among alcoholics, and they typically blame others for their problems. They are also quite sensitive and easily hurt.

The high scores that alcoholics receive on the psychopathic deviate scale of the MMPI are shared by various other drug addicts. These include abusers of narcotics, amphetamines, barbiturates, and LSD. Other addicted people who score high on this scale are heavy marijuana smokers, gamblers, and people with eating disorders.

UPI/BETTMANN NEWSPHOTOS

A man lies dead of stab wounds in the aftermath of a drunken brawl at a hobo camp in Norwood, Ohio, in the 1930s. What makes people drink excessively? Several methods of study, such as the MacAndrew Alcoholism Scale, which measures alcoholic personality characteristics, are beginning to provide possible answers to this question.

The MacAndrew Alcoholism Scale

Despite the frequency and consistency with which alcoholics and other substance abusers score high on the psychopathic deviate scale of the MMPI, high scores on this scale are by no means unique to addicts. Other people with an unconventional attitude toward life also tend to score high on the scale.

To measure alcoholic personality characteristics even more specifically, psychologist Craig MacAndrew set out to revise the MMPI scale. To do so he administered the entire MMPI (566 items) to a group of hospitalized alcoholics and a group of hospitalized nonalcoholic psychiatric patients. Comparing their answers, he found that the two groups answered 49 of the items differently (excluding 2 items that pertained directly to the misuse of alcohol). So MacAndrew wrote a new scale consisting of the same 49 items. It has come to be called the MacAndrew Alcoholism Scale, or MAC Scale. It has proven highly reliable in its ability to distinguish alcoholics from nonalcoholics.

Father and son enjoy a beer together at a bar in New York. The extent to which drinking is promoted in a person's immediate environment often determines whether that person will develop a drinking problem.

MacAndrew described people who score high on the MAC Scale as bold and aggressive "reward seekers." One of their primary concerns is to seek out and enjoy the pleasures of life. They thrive on excitement. However, it should be carefully noted that a high score on the MAC Scale is no guarantee that a person is an alcoholic. Obviously, some people with these personality characteristics do not have a problem with alcohol, and some alcoholics do not get high scores on the MAC Scale. Heroin addicts, multiple drug abusers, and smokers also score high on this scale. Thus, a person's score on the MAC Scale can not by itself be used to determine whether or not that person is an alcoholic or prone to addiction of any sort.

The Sensation Seeking Scale

The Sensation Seeking Scale, which was developed by psychologist Marvin Zuckerman, provides further information about an alcoholic's relationship to incentives.

As the name Sensation Seeking Scale implies, people who score high on this scale are drawn to excitement and new sources of stimulation. They like wild, exciting experiences—even ones that are frightening, illegal, or socially unacceptable. They are easily bored with the routine and the predictable.

High scores on the Sensation Seeking Scale also tell us a great deal about the amount and variety of an abuser's drug use. People who score high on this scale use more drugs and more different kinds of drugs than other people. High scores in sensation seeking are also achieved by smokers, people who prefer stimulating foods, and people who consume a lot of alcohol when given the chance to do so in experimental drinking situations.

To summarize, several commonly used tests demonstrate that people who exhibit various types of addictive behavior tend to have unconventional life values and a seeming indifference to society's norms and conventions. They show little remorse about violating these standards. They tend to seek immediate gratification and thrills and are unable to work toward long-range goals and rewards. This tendency extends to their relationships with other people. They are initially sociable and likeable but tend to have difficulty establishing enduring, committed relationships.

Mood and Self-esteem

Affect (mood) refers to the way people feel inside and react to the world around them. Of course, everyone's mood fluctuates from time to time and from situation to situation. Some people, though, feel a certain mood much of the time no matter what is actually going on in their lives. For example, one person might typically have little energy, find little enjoyment in the ordinary pleasures of life, and feel sad and pessimistic. Such an individual is said to be depressed. Another person might typically have great sources of energy, be involved in a variety of activities that he or she enjoys pursuing, and feel happy and optimistic much of the time; if these reactions are intense enough, the person is said to be manic.

Self-esteem refers to the way people feel about themselves—how worthy they consider themselves to be. There is usually a connection between a person's mood and feelings of self-esteem. If someone's mood is depressed, his or her self-esteem is likely to be low. This could take the form of

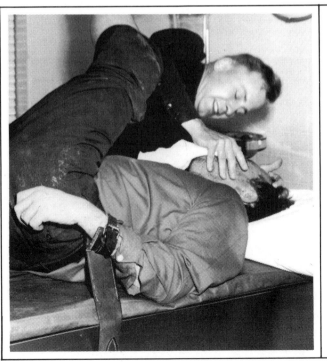

Actor Lawrence Tierney is gagged by a Los Angeles police officer. Tierney, who had been drinking, was taken to a hospital for treatment of cuts received in a brawl. He immediately began verbally abusing the emergency room nurses. Studies indicate that people with drinking problems are characteristically moody, depressed, and impulsive.

UPI/BETTMANN NEWSPHOTOS

pervasive feelings of worthlessness, diminishment, apathy, and lethargy. On the other hand, if a person's mood is elated, his or her self-esteem is likely to be high, and the person will feel positive and confident.

Pre-alcoholics show little evidence of low self-esteem. Instead, they demonstrate self-confidence, independence, and a lack of concern for what other people think of them. However, the self-esteem of pre-alcoholics changes considerably by the time their alcohol problems have become serious enough for them to seek treatment. In fact, one of the most striking characteristics of alcoholics who enter treatment is the intensity of their feelings of worthlessness. Often these feelings of worthlessness are a reflection of their dissatisfaction with the way they think they actually are as compared with the way they would like to be. Among alcoholics, low self-esteem is common to both sexes but especially prevalent among women.

Moodiness, depression, and anxiety seem to go hand in hand with the use of many psychoactive drugs. No matter how a person feels before habit formation sets in, substance abuse often results eventually in "negative affect"—a pervasive bad mood. Tests that measure "general emotionality" have consistently found that alcoholics, for example, are more emotional, tense, and worried than nonalcoholics. Tests that measure specific emotions have usually found alcoholics to be very depressed and anxious. They are tormented by unfounded worries. Moreover, there seems to be a direct correspondence between the degree of these negative feelings and the extent to which the sufferer has developed a physical dependency on the substance he or she is abusing.

In addition to studying alcoholics who are entering treatment programs, psychologists have studied the emotionality of people who are just beginning to develop problems with their drinking but are not yet alcoholics. Strong negative affect is far less common among these people than among people with more serious alcohol problems, suggesting that in the case of alcoholics the negative affect is caused by the abuse of alcohol.

There are other indications that negative affect is a consequence rather than a cause of alcoholism. For example, we saw that there was little or no indication that pre-alcoholics had negative affect. Moreover, as alcoholics go through treatment programs and continue to abstain from alcohol, their depression and anxiety are greatly reduced.

There is evidence that even moderate social drinking can cause chronic depression and anxiety. Researchers from the National Institute on Alcohol Abuse and Alcoholism and the University of California, Irvine, recently published a study in which moderate social drinkers either abstained from alcohol for a period of six weeks or continued to drink in their usual manner. The researchers found that the group of social drinkers who abstained felt a great deal better emotionally than those who continued to drink. These results suggest that the long-term effects of even moderate drinking are decidedly negative, that these negative effects influence people even when they are sober, and that they build up over time. Although these effects are subtle and people might not realize they are occurring, they are very real indeed.

Scientific studies have firmly linked excessive drinking and suicidal behavior. The 19-year-old man on top of this building in Boston came to work intoxicated and threatened to kill himself when ordered to go home. He finally collapsed and was taken into custody.

Cognitive/Perceptual Style

The term cognition refers to the ways in which people think about and organize information. The term perception refers to the ways in which they see and interpret the world around them. The styles of people's cognitive and perceptual processes are usually very similar, and that is why we consider them together.

Psychologists have administered tests to alcoholics and other substance abusers that measure their cognitive/perceptual style, and have found that their style is different from that of people who are not addicted to drugs. Three categories of tests have been used: those measuring locus of control, stimulus intensity modulation, and field dependence and independence.

Locus of Control

Locus of control is simply another way of saying "Who's in charge?" We say that locus of control is *internal* if a person feels that he or she is pretty much in control of himself or herself. On the other hand, the locus of control is said to be *external* if someone feels that forces beyond his or her control—such as luck, fate, other people, or God—determine what happens.

For the most part, it is healthier for a person to be internally controlled than externally controlled. Internally controlled people are likely to take action to manage their lives, whereas externally controlled people are likely to sit and wait for things to happen. Nevertheless, to be extreme in either direction is not good. People who are extremely internally controlled would probably be too hard on themselves, always blaming themselves for things that go wrong even when they are not really responsible.

As might be expected, studies have demonstrated that alcoholics and other drug abusers tend to feel that their lives are pretty much determined by forces beyond their control. They are easily influenced by environmental factors and do not perceive that they themselves are capable of controlling their drug use. These feelings of helplessness spill over into all aspects of their experience, leaving abusers feeling buffeted by events and emotions that they are powerless to change or even manage.

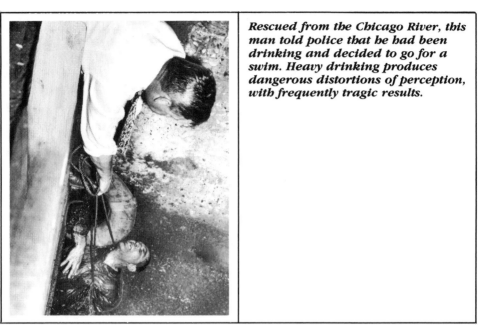

Rescued from the Chicago River, this man told police that he had been drinking and decided to go for a swim. Heavy drinking produces dangerous distortions of perception, with frequently tragic results.

A definite relationship has been found between locus of control and patterns of drinking among people in the general population. Studies investigating this relationship have placed people in different categories based on their drinking behavior. At one extreme are people who do not drink at all, and at the other are people whose drinking has caused problems. Results of these studies indicate that as the level of drinking increases, so does the degree of external control.

Stimulus Intensity Modulation

We know that response to physical pain is partly psychological. Mental attitude accounts to some extent for the fact that while some people can withstand intensely harmful stimuli without feeling much pain, others feel intense pain when experiencing relatively harmless stimuli. This is frequently borne out by natural childbirth. Women who are properly prepared and consequently relaxed and confident about labor and delivery are likely to experience much less pain than women who are fearful that their experience will be physically excruciating.

Stimulus intensity modulation involves the psychological mechanisms that come into play in a person's overall reaction to physical stimuli, especially unpleasant ones. To varying degrees, people register the intensity of stimuli subjectively. In other words, people's personalities often have as much to do with their perceptions of stimuli as the stimuli themselves. Perceived intensity may or may not correspond to actual intensity. People may modulate the actual intensity of the stimulus by perceiving it to be more or less intense than it actually is.

Augmenters are people who magnify the intensity of stimuli, *reducers* are people who minimize the intensity of stimuli, and *moderates* are people who perceive the stimuli accurately. We can determine which category a person belongs to with the Kinesthetic Aftereffect Test. People taking this test are first blindfolded and then given blocks of various sizes to examine with their fingers. When each block is removed, the subject gives his or her estimate of its size. As might be expected, augmenters overestimate the sizes of the blocks, reducers underestimate them, and moderates gauge correctly.

How is the concept of stimulus intensity modulation related to addictive behavior? The research on stimulus intensity modulation and drug addiction is not extensive, but preliminary findings suggest that the response of addicts to stimuli tends to be distorted and that they use drugs in an attempt to correct these distortions. For example, alcoholics tend to be augmenters. They use alcohol in an effort to reduce the intensity with which they experience painful and unpleasant stimuli.

Field Dependence and Independence

Field dependence and *field independence* are terms that psychologists use to describe the ways in which people organize their perceptions of the world around them. People who rely on external stimuli to form their perceptions are called field dependent. People who rely on internal stimuli are called field independent.

During the 1950s, the psychologist Herman Witkin devised several tests to measure field dependence and field independence. Witkin thought that a person's perceptual style was related to his or her basic personality characteristics and that laboratory tests measuring perceptual processes might provide a convenient way to study the interrelationships between perception and personality. The tests developed by Witkin were the Body Adjustment Test, the Rod and Frame Test, and the Embedded Figures Test. A brief description of these tests will be helpful in explaining the complex concept of field dependence and independence.

In the Body Adjustment Test, the subject is seated in an adjustable chair that is suspended inside a small experimental room that can be moved by the test administrator to various angles while the subject's chair remains stationary. After the test administrator moves the room, the person taking the test is asked to adjust the chair to a perfectly upright position. Field independent people are able to align the chair to a near-perfect upright position. On the other hand, field dependent people perform the test inaccurately. Their perceptual judgments are distorted by the position of the surrounding room.

In the Rod and Frame Test, the subject is placed in a dark room where he or she views an illuminated rod that is surrounded by an illuminated rectangular frame. Both the rod and the frame can be arranged at different angles by the

Dr. E. M. Jellinek, who worked closely with Alcoholics Anonymous, helped promote the idea of alcoholism as a special kind of allergic reaction. Dr. Jellinek, a Yale University physiologist, theorized that alcoholics have less tolerance for alcohol than other people, and that as little as one drink can cause them to lose control.

test administrator. The subject is asked to adjust the rod so that it is in a perfectly upright position, regardless of the position the frame is in. Again, field independent people are able to perform this task accurately, while field dependent people have difficulty doing so, since their judgments are influenced by the position of the surrounding frame.

The Embedded Figures Test consists of a series of pictures that have other pictures disguised inside them. For example, faces of people or animals might be hidden within a more complex figure or scene. Field dependent people have difficulty finding the embedded figures, while field independent people can do so easily.

As might be expected, alcoholics who take such tests often demonstrate extreme field dependence. The next step is to determine whether field dependence is a cause or a consequence of alcoholism. In spite of the absence of definitive data, current researchers strongly believe that an alcoholic's field dependence is a part of the general cognitive style that was present before the onset of alcohol problems and contributed to their development. One of the ways this style presents itself is in an inability to plan ahead adequately and to realize the consequences of one's actions.

Alcoholic Personality Subtypes

The conclusions about alcohol personality characteristics described above were derived largely from studies of male alcoholics undergoing treatment. These alcoholics might represent a substantial proportion of alcoholics, but it would be a mistake to assume that the conclusions drawn from this sample necessarily apply to all alcoholics. Moreover, calculating average scores might give a false impression of what individual personalities are like.

Recognizing these possibilities for distortion, researchers have begun to concentrate their attention on *alcoholic personality subtypes*. The procedure for identifying subtypes has been to administer the MMPI or some other personality inventory and then, using sophisticated statistical procedures, to group together alcoholics whose personality characteristics are similar. Although a number of subtypes have been identified in this manner, only two subtypes have been found repeatedly.

One of these subtypes consists of "distressed, neurotic" alcoholics. They appear to drink excessively in an attempt to cope with their personal distress and psychological discomfort. They are heavy drinkers who have many problems associated with their drinking. Many of these problem drinkers use alcohol and other psychoactive drugs as a form of self-medication, mistakenly feeling that getting high will help them cope with depression, anxiety, and other negative feelings.

The second subtype consists of "sociopathic" alcoholics. Their excessive drinking appears to be part of a general and impulsive search for immediate gratification of all sorts. Such people tend to drink more moderately and have fewer problems associated with their drinking than distressed, neurotic alcoholics. They also tend to suffer fewer feelings of guilt, shame, and remorse about their drinking than do "distressed, neurotic" problem drinkers.

The identification of such addictive personality subtypes has practical implications for the treatment and prevention of alcoholism and other addictions. For instance, it would be very helpful to be able to match particular subtypes of alcoholics with the treatment technique most likely to be effective. Researchers have made some preliminary progress toward this end.

L'Absinthe *by Edgar Degas depicts two people drinking in a café. The question of whether alcohol actually reduces tension and anxiety has inspired studies and experiments on both humans and animals.*

CHAPTER 5

THE EFFECTS OF ALCOHOL ON PERSONALITY

It is very important to identify the precise effects that a drug has on personality characteristics in order to understand exactly why people use and abuse it. Researchers have devoted much attention to identifying these effects through controlled laboratory research. Because of the ethical and legal difficulties involved in the experimental use of psychoactive drugs, this research has been pretty much confined to the study of alcohol.

Researchers have been most interested in determining the effect of alcohol on people's mood. This is because there is a widely held belief that alcohol reduces negative moods, especially tension and anxiety. The fact that many people believe that alcohol reduces tension is self-evident. "I need a drink!" is a classic exclamation to announce the need to relax, and crowded bars the world over provide ample evidence that a couple of stiff drinks are regarded as the universal cure for everyday anxieties and stress. Anthropologists have found that societies with the highest levels of tension and unrest also have the highest rates of alcohol consumption. For their part, many psychoanalysts maintain that heavy drinkers use alcohol as a way of managing the extreme tension caused by the dependence/independence conflict discussed earlier. But does alcohol *really* reduce tension? Research on both animals and humans has produced some surprising results.

Early Research with Animals

During the 1940s and 1950s, the tension-reducing properties of alcohol were tested in controlled laboratory research with rats. In these experiments, the rats were typically placed in a conflict situation and then given alcohol to see if it enabled them to resolve the conflict. For example, one procedure was to train hungry rats to run through a maze in order to get a reward of food at the end. After the rat had learned this response, the experimenter then delivered an electric shock to its feet at the very moment when it was eating the food it had found.

Since now the rat was both attracted to and repelled by the food at the end of the maze, it was in conflict about running to the end of the maze. Thus, the rat behaved as if it both wanted the food and wanted to avoid the electric shock. It would run approximately halfway through the maze and then stop and slowly vacillate back and forth, as if it couldn't make up its mind whether or not to go farther. However, if the rat was then injected with alcohol, it would approach the end of the maze more closely and perhaps even eat the food. These findings were taken as evidence that alcohol had served to resolve conflict.

On the basis of such studies, psychologists developed what they called the "tension-reduction hypothesis" of alcohol consumption. The hypothesis stated not only that al-

AP/WIDE WORLD PHOTOS

Laboratory studies with rats in the 1940s and 1950s appeared to support the proposition that people drink to resolve tension. The rats in this picture were administered an electric shock every time they began eating. As a result, they were often indecisive as to whether to continue eating at the risk of receiving a shock. However, when injected with alcohol, the rats resumed eating.

cohol does reduce tension but also that people drink to reduce tension. This hypothesis prevailed for many years and was the basis of later studies on humans that were designed to test the effect of alcohol on tension.

Early Research with Humans

In the 1960s researchers began to perform experiments about the nature of alcohol on human subjects. They did so with an eye to testing all the assumptions that had for decades prevailed on the basis of the tension-reduction hypothesis. These experiments, which were performed mostly on alcoholics, were structured in a number of different ways, but they all pointed to the same general conclusion. Contrary to long-held assumptions, the relationship between tension reduction and alcohol consumption was ultimately a negative one.

At the very beginning of a drinking session, alcohol tended to make the alcoholic feel better emotionally. However, as the person continued to drink, feelings of tension and depression set in. As the drinking continued, these feelings only intensified. Of course, all of this raised serious questions about why people persist in drinking even though it makes them feel worse instead of better.

Recent Research with Humans

Originally focusing on alcoholic subjects, research on the connection between mood and alcohol consumption in human subjects has in recent years branched out to include moderate or "social" drinkers as well. There are indications that alcohol has a wide variety of effects on people's emotional reactions. It can serve to enhance positive emotions, soothe negative emotions, or intensify negative emotions. These reactions are by no means haphazard; there is a definite link between the ways in which alcohol affects particular people at particular times and the specific circumstances under which the alcohol is consumed.

Of course, the amount of alcohol consumed has a great deal to do with the effect it has on the drinker. Small quantities—for example, one or two drinks—are more likely to cause positive emotional reactions than larger quantities. Larger quantities often cause negative emotional reactions, such as tension, irritability, hostility, and depression. (The precise point at which the scales begin to tip will vary according to such things as the body weight, metabolism, and state of mind of the individual drinker.)

Blood alcohol level (the amount of alcohol in a person's bloodstream) also plays a crucial role in determining how alcohol will affect a drinker's mood at any given time. During any drinking occasion, the blood alcohol level rises until it reaches a peak and then falls slowly again as the alcohol is metabolized from the bloodstream. For any given blood alcohol concentration that we consider, we can find a point on the descending blood-alcohol-concentration curve that exactly corresponds to a point on the ascending part of the curve. Although people will have the same amount of alcohol in their bloodstream at these two points, the alcohol will affect them very differently depending upon whether the level of alcohol is increasing or decreasing. A person is more likely to feel happy, relaxed, and carefree if his or her blood alcohol level is rising . If it is falling, the person is more likely to feel gloomy, belligerent, or tearful.

Where and under what circumstances alcohol is consumed also influences its effects. In a pleasant, party-like environment, drinking is more likely to contribute to a person's emotional well-being. In a drab, isolated laboratory environment, alcohol may actually make a person feel worse rather than better.

Gender also plays an important role in the effect of alcohol on mood. In one study, men and women drank alcohol together in a relaxed, friendly setting. At the beginning and at the end of the "party," they were given a test to measure how they felt about themselves. Whereas the self-regard of the men was greater after drinking, the self-esteem of the women had been undermined. Perhaps alcohol typically affects men and women differently because of society's double standard about drinking. While men are encouraged to drink—even to drink heavily—as a sign of manliness, drinking among women (especially heavy drinking and intoxication) is strongly frowned upon.

In spite of the actual effects that alcohol has on people's emotions, the illusion that its effects are exclusively positive persists. When both alcoholics and social drinkers are asked to list the effects they expect alcohol to have on them, they usually mention only positive consequences, such as relaxation, heightened enjoyment of food and conversation, and increased self-esteem. It is as if drinkers only remember the happy glow induced by the first few drinks, stubbornly blotting out all the unpleasant realities of the intoxication and the resulting hangover.

The Role of Alcohol in Controlling Positive Emotions

As we have seen, people use alcohol to enhance or hold on to pleasant feelings as well as to ease unpleasant ones. Among people who develop drinking problems, the use of alcohol as a positive reinforcer seems most prominent in the early stages of their drinking (remember that the pre-alcoholic tends to be more independent, gregarious, and impulsive than other people and does not typically suffer from such afflictions as depression, anxiety, and low self-esteem).

We have also seen that from the outset alcohol affects the emotions of people who are more likely to develop problems than people who are not likely to be at risk. When

It is not uncommon for acute alcoholics who abruptly give up drinking to suffer from delirium tremens or DTs. Symptoms of this withdrawal syndrome include hallucinations, delusions, and elevated blood pressure.

alcoholics report the effect that alcohol had on them when they first started drinking, they often remember their experiences as profoundly reinforcing, even euphoric. These people derive a special high from drinking that other people apparently do not experience.

The informal accounts of problem drinkers have been substantiated by controlled laboratory research. There is strong evidence to suggest that people who eventually develop drinking problems have a unique reaction to alcohol. Future problem drinkers seem to use alcohol to enhance their good feelings rather than to counteract negative ones.

The Role of Alcohol in Controlling Negative Emotions

As future alcoholics continue to drink more and more heavily, significant changes occur in their emotional lives. Alcohol gradually becomes more important as a means of controlling negative emotions. Changes occur in the feelings that alcohol produces in a person's overall state of mind, whether the person is drinking or not at any given time. The negative effects of alcohol begin to be pervasive and critically undermine whatever motivation the problem drinker might otherwise have to improve the deteriorating conditions of his or her life through nonchemical means.

One important reason why the effects of alcohol on the habitual heavy drinker change over time has to do with the defenses the body develops to process the toxins (poison) in alcohol. This involves the physical tolerance of alcohol discussed earlier. Ever-increasing amounts of alcohol are required to get high, thus making it more and more difficult to recreate the positive feelings the alcohol once induced.

Ironically, heavy drinking over time produces both chronic anxiety and depression, which the alcoholic then attempts to "treat" by drinking even more. By the time this vicious cycle is firmly established, the alcoholic will probably require some form of treatment if he or she is to be weaned from this dependence on alcohol.

Unfortunately, many alcoholics—however bad they may be feeling—persist in denying that alcohol has become the cause of their woes or that it has any negative effect on them at all. Many alcoholics have literally ruined themselves—lost marriages, jobs, homes, friends—and still cannot bring themselves to admit that they must stop drinking before they can be helped.

The dynamics of denial are perhaps the most mysterious aspect of addiction. They are also the most difficult to treat. Once any psychoactive substance (including alcohol) has become central in a person's life, the prospect of giving it up seems both threatening and overwhelmingly difficult. Obviously, if life without a drug such as alcohol, cocaine, or marijuana seems impossible, the addict has a great investment in denying that the drug has become a destructive force in his or her life. Tragically, once addiction has set in, even people who know deep down that substance abuse has become the heart of their difficulties engage in elaborate rationalizations and self-delusions to avoid facing this fact.

The long-term negative effects of alcohol and other psychoactive substances on even social drinkers or moderate users are now well documented. Whether people use psychoactive drugs moderately or to excess, it has been shown that their state of mind improves measurably when they remain completely drug-free for a period of at least six weeks or more.

VICTORIA TOMASELLI

Individuals suffering from depression, one of the 10 clinical scales of the Minnesota Multiphasic Personality Inventory, are often afflicted with feelings of self-hatred.

Many people drink to reduce the intensity of unpleasant experiences, but a life of pain and despair is frequently the fate of untreated alcoholics. Here, two men share a bottle in a New York City alley.

CHAPTER 6

CONCLUSIONS

*T*here is no single explanation as to why some people are more vulnerable to addiction than others. The evidence indicates that alcoholics and other substance abusers have personality characteristics that distinguish them from non-addicted individuals, that the distinctive personality characteristics of alcoholics were apparent even before they began to abuse substances, and that initially alcohol and other drugs have special reinforcing effects on people who subsequently develop substance-abuse problems. The uniquely euphoric and relaxing effect that alcohol and other drugs have on potential abusers helps to explain in part why they continue to use these substances to excess. This dynamic is particularly true in cases of cocaine and heroin abuse.

As far as pre-addictive personality characteristics are concerned, pre-alcoholics tend to be independent and gregarious. However, such people have great difficulty forming meaningful, intimate relationships with others. They do things impulsively, are unable to tolerate frustration, reject the traditional values of society, and are unable to sacrifice immediate gratification in the interest of working toward long-range goals. In contrast to abusers of hard drugs, people with alcohol problems do not seem to suffer from low self-esteem, depression, or anxiety before the debilitating chemical effects of alcohol take over. People with addictive tendencies are apt to feel that they do not have much control over the circumstances of their own lives, and they tend to be much more sensitive to all forms of stimulation than do people with nonaddictive tendencies. They seek easy thrills and excitement and do not seem to get much satisfaction from ordinary experience.

Once addiction to alcohol or other drugs has set in, its victims are trapped in a vicious cycle of depression, anxiety, and low self-esteem which they futilely and self-destructively attempt to manage by using ever-increasing amounts of the substance that caused so many problems in the first place. Denial, coupled with a dread of the difficulties of withdrawal and the physical dynamics of tolerance and dependence, makes all forms of addiction very difficult to treat.

Appendix I

POPULATION ESTIMATES OF LIFETIME AND CURRENT NONMEDICAL DRUG USE, 1988

	12-17 years (pop. 20,250,000)				18-25 years (pop. 29,688,000)			
	%	Ever Used	%	Current User	%	Ever Used	%	Current User
Marijuana & Hashish	17	3,516,000	6	1,296,000	56	16,741,000	16	4,594,000
Hallucinogens	3	704,000	1	168,000	14	4,093,000	2	569,000
Inhalants	9	1,774,000	2	410,000	12	3,707,000	2	514,000
Cocaine	3	683,000	1	225,000	20	5,858,000	5	1,323,000
Crack	1	188,000	+	+	3	1,000,000	1	249,000
Heroin	1	118,000	+	+	+	+	+	+
Stimulants*	4	852,000	1	245,000	1	3,366,000	2	718,000
Sedatives	2	475,000	1	1 23,000	6	1,633,000	1	265,000
Tranquilizers	2	413,000	+	+	8	2,319,000	1	307,000
Analgesics	4	840,000	1	182,000	9	2,798,000	1	440,000
Alcohol	50	10,161,000	25	5,097,000	90	26,807,000	65	19,392,000
Cigarettes	42	8,564,000	12	2,389,000	75	22,251,000	35	10,447,000
Smokeless Tobacco	15	3,021,000	4	722,000	24	6,971,000	6	1,855,000

* Amphetamines and related substances
+ Amounts of less than .5% are not listed
  Terms: Ever Used: used at least once in a person's lifetime.
  Current User: used at least once in the 30 days prior to the survey.

Source: National Institute on Drug Abuse, August 1989

POPULATION ESTIMATES OF LIFETIME AND CURRENT
NONMEDICAL DRUG USE, 1988

26+ years (pop. 148,409,000)				TOTAL (pop. 198,347,000)			
%	Ever Used	%	Current User	%	Ever Used	%	Current User
31	45,491,000	4	5,727,000	33	65,748,000	6	11,616,000
7	9,810,000	+	+	7	4,607,000	+	+
4	5,781,000	+	+	6	1,262,000	1	1,223,000
10	14,631,000	1	1,375,000	11	21,171,000	2	2,923,000
+	+	+	+	1	2,483,000	+	484,000
1	1,686,000	+	+	1	1,907,000	+	+
7	9,850,000	1	791,000	7	4,068,000	1	1,755,000
3	4,867,000	+	+	4	6,975,000	+	+
5	6,750,000	1	822,000	5	9,482,000	1	1,174,000
5	6,619,000	+	+	5	10,257,000	1	1,151,000
89	131,530,000	55	81,356,000	85	168,498,000	53	105,845,000
80	118,191,000	30	44,284,000	75	149,005,000	29	57,121,000
13	19,475,000	3	4,497,000	15	29,467,000	4	7,073,000

Appendix II

DRUGS MENTIONED MOST FREQUENTLY BY HOSPITAL EMERGENCY ROOMS, 1988

	Drug name	Number of mentions by emergency rooms	Percent of total number of mentions
1	Cocaine	62,141	38.80
2	Alcohol-in-combination	46,588	29.09
3	Heroin/Morphine	20,599	12.86
4	Marijuana/Hashish	10,722	6.69
5	PCP/PCP Combinations	8,403	5.25
6	Acetaminophen	6,426	4.01
7	Diazepam	6,082	3.80
8	Aspirin	5,544	3.46
9	Ibuprofen	3,878	2.42
10	Alprazolam	3,846	2.40
11	Methamphetamine/Speed	3,030	1.89
12	Acetaminophen W Codeine	2,457	1.53
13	Amitriptyline	1,960	1.22
14	D.T.C. Sleep Aids	1,820	1.14
15	Methadone	1,715	1.07
16	Triazolam	1,640	1.02
17	Diphenhydramine	1,574	0.98
18	D-Propoxyphene	1,563	0.98
19	Hydantoin	1,442	0.90
20	Lorazepam	1,345	0.84
21	LSD	1,317	0.82
22	Amphetamine	1,316	0.82
23	Phenobarbital	1,223	0.76
24	Oxycodone	1,192	0.74
25	Imipramine	1,064	0.66

Source: Drug Abuse Warning Network (DAWN), Annual Data 1988

Appendix III

DRUGS MENTIONED MOST FREQUENTLY BY MEDICAL EXAMINERS
(IN AUTOPSY REPORTS), 1988

	Drug name	Number of mentions in autopsy reports	Percent of total number of drug mentions
1	Cocaine	3,308	48.96
2	Alcohol-in-combination	2,596	38.43
3	Heroin/Morphine	2,480	36.71
4	Codeine	689	10.20
5	Diazepam	464	6.87
6	Methadone	447	6.62
7	Amitriptyline	402	5.95
8	Nortriptyline	328	4.85
9	Lidocaine	306	4.53
10	Acetaminophen	293	4.34
11	D-Propoxyphene	271	4.01
12	Marijuana/Hashish	263	3.89
13	Quinine	224	3.32
14	Unspec Benzodiazepine	222	3.29
15	PCP/PCP Combinations	209	3.09
16	Diphenhydramine	192	2.84
17	Phenobarbital	183	2.71
18	Desipramine	177	2.62
19	Methamphetamine/Speed	161	2.38
20	Doxepin	152	2.25
21	Aspirin	138	2.04
22	Imipramine	137	2.03
23	Hydantoin	98	1.45
24	Amphetamine	87	1.29
25	Chlordiazepoxide	76	1.12

Source: Drug Abuse Warning Network (DAWN), <u>Annual Data 1988</u>

Appendix IV

NATIONAL HIGH SCHOOL SENIOR SURVEY, 1975-1989

	High School Senior Survey Trends in Lifetime Prevalence Percent Who Ever Used				
	Class of 1975	Class of 1976	Class of 1977	Class of 1978	Class of 1979
Marijuana/Hashish	47.3	52.8	56.4	59.2	60.4
Inhalants	NA	10.3	11.1	12.0	12.7
Inhalants Adjusted	NA	NA	NA	NA	18.2
Amyl & Butyl Nitrites	NA	NA	NA	NA	11.1
Hallucinogens	16.3	15.1	13.9	14.3	14.1
Hallucinogens Adjusted	NA	NA	NA	NA	17.7
LSD	11.3	11.0	9.8	9.7	9.5
PCP	NA	NA	NA	NA	12.8
Cocaine	9.0	9.7	10.8	12.9	15.4
Crack	NA	NA	NA	NA	NA
Other cocaine	NA	NA	NA	NA	NA
Heroin	2.2	1.8	1.8	1.6	1.1
Other Opiates*	9.0	9.6	10.3	9.9	10.1
Stimulants*	22.3	22.6	23.0	22.9	24.2
Stimulants Adjusted*	NA	NA	NA	NA	NA
Sedatives*	18.2	17.7	17.4	16.0	14.6
Barbiturates*	16.9	16.2	15.6	13.7	11.8
Methaqualone*	8.1	7.8	8.5	7.9	8.3
Tranquilizers*	17.0	16.8	18.0	17.0	16.3
Alcohol	90.4	91.9	92.5	93.1	93.0
Cigarettes	73.6	75.4	75.7	75.3	74.0

Stimulants adjusted to exclude inappropriate reporting of nonprescription stimulants; stimulants = amphetamines and amphetamine-like substances.
*Only use not under a doctor's orders included.

Source: National Institute on Drug Abuse, National High School Senior Survey: "Monitoring the Future," 1989

NATIONAL HIGH SCHOOL SENIOR SURVEY, 1975-1989

High School Senior Survey
Trends in Lifetime Prevalence
Percent Who Ever Used

Class of 1980	Class of 1981	Class of 1982	Class of 1983	Class of 1984	Class of 1985	Class of 1986	Class of 1987	Class of 1988	Class of 1989
60.3	59.5	58.7	57.0	54.9	54.2	50.9	50.2	47.2	43.7
11.9	12.3	12.8	13.6	14.4	15.4	15.9	17.0	16.7	17.6
17.3	17.2	17.7	18.2	18.0	18.1	20.1	18.6	17.5	18.6
11.1	10.1	9.8	8.4	8.1	7.9	8.6	4.7	3.2	3.3
13.3	13.3	12.5	11.9	10.7	10.3	9.7	10.3	8.9	9.4
15.6	15.3	14.3	13.6	12.3	12.1	11.9	10.6	9.2	9.9
9.3	9.8	9.6	8.9	8.0	7.5	7.2	8.4	7.7	8.3
9.6	7.8	6.0	5.6	5.0	4.9	4.8	3.0	2.9	3.9
15.7	16.5	16.0	16.2	16.1	17.3	16.9	15.2	12.1	10.3
NA	NA	NA	NA	NA	NA	NA	5.4	4.8	4.7
NA	NA	NA	NA	NA	NA	NA	14.0	12.1	8.5
1.1	1.1	1.2	1.2	1.3	1.2	1.1	1.2	1.1	1.3
9.8	10.1	9.6	9.4	9.7	10.2	9.0	9.2	8.6	8.3
26.4	32.2	35.6	35.4	NA	NA	NA	NA	NA	NA
NA	NA	27.9	26.9	27.9	26.2	23.4	21.6	19.8	19.1
14.9	16.0	15.2	14.4	13.3	11.8	10.4	8.7	7.8	7.4
11.0	11.3	10.3	9.9	9.9	9.2	8.4	7.4	6.7	6.5
9.5	10.6	10.7	10.1	8.3	6.7	5.2	4.0	3.3	2.7
15.2	14.7	14.0	13.3	12.4	11.9	10.9	10.9	9.4	7.6
93.2	92.6	92.8	92.6	92.6	92.2	91.3	92.2	92.0	90.7
71.0	71.0	70.1	70.6	69.7	68.8	67.6	67.2	66.4	65.7

Appendix V

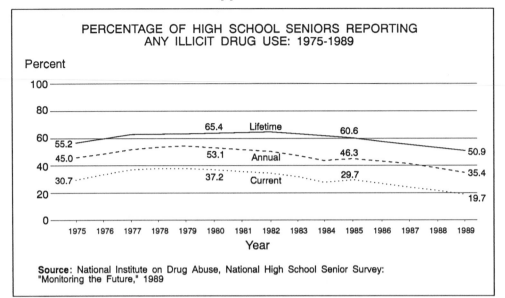

PERCENTAGE OF HIGH SCHOOL SENIORS REPORTING
ANY ILLICIT DRUG USE: 1975-1989

Percent

Source: National Institute on Drug Abuse, National High School Senior Survey: "Monitoring the Future," 1989

Appendix VI

DRUG ABUSE AND AIDS

An estimated 25 percent of all cases of acquired immunodeficiency syndrome, or AIDS, are intravenous (IV) drug abusers. This group is the second largest at risk for AIDS, exceeded only by homosexual, and bisexual men. And the numbers may be growing. Data for the first half of 1988 show that IV drug abusers made up about 31 percent of the total reported cases.

". . . the number of IV drug users with AIDS is doubling every 14-16 months."

According to the National Institute on Drug Abuse (NIDA). There are 1.1 to 1.3 million IV drug users in the United States, and, so far, about 17,500 have developed AIDS. Thousands more are infected with the virus that causes this fatal illness, which kills by destroying the body's ability to fight disease.

Currently, the number of IV drug users with AIDS is doubling every 14-16 months. Although the numbers of IV drug users who carry the AIDS virus varies from region to region, in some places the majority may already be infected. In New York City, for example, 60 percent of IV drug users entering treatment programs have the AIDS virus.

Among IV drug abusers, the AIDS virus is spread primarily by needle sharing. As long as IV drug abusers are drug dependent, they are likely to engage in needle sharing. Thus, the key to eliminating needle sharing—and the associated spread of AIDS—is drug abuse treatment to curb drug dependence. NIDA is working to find ways to get more IV users into treatment and to develop new methods to fight drug addiction.

Most non-drug users characteristically associate heroin with IV drug use. However, thousands of others inject cocaine or amphetamines. Recent evidence suggests that IV cocaine use is increasing and that the AIDS virus is spreading in those users. One reason for this may be because cocaine's effects last only a short time. When the drug, which is a stimulant, wears off, users may inject again and again, sharing a needle many times in a few hours. In contrast, heroin users inject once and fall asleep.

". . . IV cocaine use is increasing and the AIDS
virus is spreading in those users."

The apparent increase in IV cocaine is especially worrisome, drug abuse experts say, because there are no standard therapies for treating cocaine addiction. Until scientists find effective treatments for this problem, the ability to control the spread of AIDS will be hampered.

TRANSMISSION

Needle Sharing -- Among IV drug users, transmission of AIDS virus most often occurs by sharing needles, syringes, or other "works." Small amounts of contaminated blood left in the equipment can carry the virus from user to user. IV drug abusers who frequent "shooting galleries" — where paraphernalia is passed among several people -- are at especially high risk for AIDS. But, needle sharing of any sort (at parties, for example) can transmit the virus, and NIDA experts note that almost all IV drug users share needles at one time or another.

Because not every IV drug abuser will enter treatment and because some must wait to be treated, IV users in many cities are being taught to flush their "works" with bleach before they inject. Used correctly, bleach can destroy virus left in the equipment.

Sexual Transmission -- IV drug abusers also get AIDS through unprotected sex with someone who is infected. In addition, the AIDS virus can be sexually transmitted from infected IV drug abusers to individuals who do not use drugs. Data from the Centers for Disease Control show that IV drug use is associated with the increased spread of AIDS in the heterosexual population. For example, of all women reported to have AIDS, 49 percent were IV drug users, while another 30 percent -- non-IV drug users themselves -- were sexual partners of IV drug users. Infected women who become pregnant can pass the AIDS virus to their babies. About 70 percent of all children born with AIDS have had a mother or father who shot drugs.

Non-IV Drug Use and AIDS -- Sexual activity has also been reported as the means of AIDS transmission among those who use non-IV drugs (like crack or marijuana). Many people, especially women, addicted to crack (or other substances) go broke supporting their habit and turn to trading sex for drugs. Another link between substance abuse and AIDS is when individuals using alcohol and drugs relax their restraints and caution regarding sexual behavior. People who normally practice "safe" sex may neglect to do so while "under the influence."

Source: U.S. Public Health Service, AIDS Program Office, 1989

Appendix VII

U.S. Drug Schedules*

	Drugs Included	Dispensing Regulations
Schedule I high potential for abuse; no currently accepted medical use in treatment in U.S.; safety not proven for medical use	heroin methaqualone LSD mescaline peyote phencyclidine analogs psilocybin marijuana hashish	research use only
Schedule II high potential for abuse; currently accepted U.S. medical use; abuse may lead to severe psychological or physical dependence	opium morphine methadone barbiturates cocaine amphetamines phencyclidine codeine	written Rx; no refills
Schedule III less potential for abuse than drugs in Schedules I and II; currently accepted U.S. medical use; may lead to moderate or low physical dependence or high psychological dependence	glutethimide selected morphine, opium, and codeine compounds selected depressant sedative compounds selected stimulants for weight control	written or oral Rx; refills allowed
Schedule IV low potential for abuse relative to drugs in Schedule III; currently accepted U.S. medical use; abuse may lead to limited physical dependence or psychological dependence relative to drugs in Schedule III	selected barbiturate and other depressant compounds selected stimulants for weight control	written or oral Rx; refills allowed
Schedule V low potential for abuse relative to drugs in Schedule IV; currently accepted U.S. medical use; abuse may lead to limited physical dependence or psychological dependence relative to drugs in Schedule IV	selected narcotic compounds	OTC/ M.D.'s order

*Established by the U.S. Controlled Substances Act of 1970
Source: U.S. Drug Enforcement Administration

Appendix VIII

Agencies for the Prevention and Treatment of Drug Abuse

UNITED STATES

Alabama
Department of Mental Health
Division of Substance Abuse
200 Interstate Park Drive
P.O. Box 3710
Montgomery, AL 36109
(205) 270-9650

Alaska
Department of Health and
   Social Services
Division of Alcoholism and
   Drug Abuse
P.O. Box H
Juneau, AK 99811-0607
(907) 586-6201

Arizona
Department of Health
   Services
Division of Behavioral Health
   Services
Bureau of Community
   Services
The Office of Substance
   Abuse
2632 East Thomas
Phoenix, AZ 85016
(602) 255-1030

Arkansas
Department of Human
   Services
Division of Alcohol and Drug
   Abuse
400 Donagy Plaza North
P.O. Box 1437
Slot 2400
Little Rock, AR 72203-1437
(501) 682-6656

California
Health and Welfare Agencies
Department of Alcohol and
   Drug Programs
1700 K Street
Sacramento, CA 95814-4037
(916) 445-1943

Colorado
Department of Health
Alcohol and Drug Abuse
   Division
4210 East 11th Avenue
Denver, CO 80220
(303) 331-8201

Connecticut
Alcohol and Drug Abuse
   Commission
999 Asylum Avenue
3rd Floor
Hartford, CT 06105
(203) 566-4145

Delaware
Division of Mental Health
Bureau of Alcoholism and
   Drug Abuse
1901 North Dupont Highway
Newcastle, DE 19720
(302) 421-6101

District of Columbia
Department of Human
   Services
Office of Health Planning and
   Development
1660 L Street NW
Room 715
Washington, DC 20036
(202) 724-5641

Florida
Department of Health and
   Rehabilitative Services
Alcohol, Drug Abuse, and
   Mental Health Office
1317 Winewood Boulevard
Building 6, Room 183
Tallahassee, FL 32399-0700
(904) 488-8304

Georgia
Department of Human
   Resources
Division of Mental Health,
   Mental Retardation, and
   Substance Abuse
Alcohol and Drug Section
878 Peachtree Street
Suite 319
Atlanta, GA 30309-3917
(404) 894-4785

Hawaii
Department of Health
Mental Health Division
Alcohol and Drug Abuse
   Branch
1270 Queen Emma Street
Room 706
Honolulu, HI 96813
(808) 548-4280

Idaho
Department of Health and
   Welfare
Bureau of Preventive
   Medicine
Substance Abuse Section
450 West State
Boise, ID 83720
(208) 334-5934

Illinois
Department of Alcoholism
   and Substance Abuse
Illinois Center
100 West Randolph Street
Suite 5-600
Chicago, IL 60601
(312) 814-3840

Indiana
Department of Mental Health
Division of Addiction Services
117 East Washington Street
Indianapolis, IN 46204-3647
(317) 232-7816

Iowa
Department of Public Health
Division of Substance Abuse
Lucas State Office Building
321 East 12th Street
Des Moines, IA 50319
(515) 281-3641

Kansas
Department of Social
  Rehabilitation
Alcohol and Drug Abuse
  Services
300 SW Oakley
2nd Floor
Biddle Building
Topeka, KS 66606
(913) 296-3925

Kentucky
Cabinet for Human Resources
Department of Health
  Services
Substance Abuse Branch
275 East Main Street
Frankfort, KY 40621
(502) 564-2880

Louisiana
Department of Health and
  Hospitals
Office of Human Services
Division of Alcohol and Drug
  Abuse
P.O. Box 3868
Baton Rouge, LA 70821-3868
1201 Capital Access Road
Baton Rouge, LA 70802
(504) 342-9354

Maine
Department of Human
  Services
Office of Alcoholism and
  Drug Abuse Prevention
Bureau of Rehabilitation
5 Anthony Avenue
State House, Station 11
Augusta, ME 04433
(207) 289-2781

Maryland
Alcohol and Drug Abuse
  Administration
201 West Preston Street

4th Floor
Baltimore, MD 21201
(301) 225-6910

Massachusetts
Department of Public Health
Division of Substance Abuse
150 Tremont Street
Boston, MA 02111
(617) 727-1960

Michigan
Department of Public Health
Office of Substance Abuse
  Services
2150 Apollo Drive
P.O. Box 30206
Lansing, MI 48909
(517) 335-8810

Minnesota
Department of Human
  Services
Chemical Dependency
  Division
444 Lafayette Road
St. Paul, MN 55155
(612) 296-4614

Mississippi
Department of Mental Health
Division of Alcohol and Drug
  Abuse
1101 Robert E. Lee Building
239 North Lamar Street
Jackson, MS 39201
(601) 359-1288

Missouri
Department of Mental
  Health
Division of Alcoholism and
  Drug Abuse
1706 East Elm Street
P.O. Box 687
Jefferson City, MO 65102
(314) 751-4942

Montana
Department of Institutions
Alcohol and Drug Abuse
  Division
1539 11th Avenue
Helena, MT 59620
(406) 444-2827

Nebraska
Department of Public
  Institutions
Division of Alcoholism and
  Drug Abuse
801 West Van Dorn Street
P.O. Box 94728
Lincoln, NB 68509-4728
(402) 471-2851, Ext. 5583

Nevada
Department of Human
  Resources
Bureau of Alcohol and Drug
  Abuse
505 East King Street
Room 500
Carson City, NV 89710
(702) 687-4790

New Hampshire
Department of Health and
  Human Services
Office of Alcohol and Drug
  Abuse Prevention
State Office
Park South
105 Pleasant Street
Concord, NH 03301
(603) 271-6100

New Jersey
Department of Health
Division of Alcoholism and
  Drug Abuse
129 East Hanover Street CN
  362
Trenton, NJ 08625
(609) 292-8949

New Mexico
Health and Environment
  Department
Behavioral Health Services
  Division/
Substance Abuse
Harold Runnels Building
1190 Saint Francis Drive
Santa Fe, NM 87503
(505) 827-2601

New York
Division of Alcoholism and
  Alcohol Abuse
194 Washington Avenue

Albany, NY 12210
(518) 474-5417

Division of Substance Abuse
Services
Executive Park South
Box 8200
Albany, NY 12203
(518) 457-7629

North Carolina
Department of Human
  Resources
Division of Mental Health,
  Developmental Disabilities,
  and Substance Abuse
  Services
Alcohol and Drug Abuse
  Services
325 North Salisbury Street
Albemarle Building
Raleigh, NC 27603
(919) 733-4670

North Dakota
Department of Human
  Services
Division of Alcohol and Drug
  Abuse
1839 East Capital Avenue
Bismarck, ND 58501-2152
(701) 224-2769

Ohio
Division of Alcohol and Drug
  Addiction Services
246 North High Street
Columbus, OH 43266-0170
(614) 466-3445

Oklahoma
Department of Mental Health
  and Substance Abuse
  Services
Alcohol and Drug Abuse
  Services
1200 North East 13th Street
P.O. Box 53277
Oklahoma City, OK 73152-
  3277
(405) 271-8653

Oregon
Department of Human
  Resources

Office of Alcohol and Drug
  Abuse Programs
1178 Chemeketa NE
#102
Salem, OR 97310
(503) 378-2163

Pennsylvania
Department of Health
Office of Drug and Alcohol
  Programs
Health and Welfare Building
Room 809
P.O. Box 90
Harrisburg, PA 17108
(717) 787-9857

Rhode Island
Department of Mental Health,
  Mental Retardation and
  Hospitals
Division of Substance Abuse
Substance Abuse
  Administration Building
P.O. Box 20363
Cranston, RI 02920
(401) 464-2091

South Carolina
Commission on Alcohol and
  Drug Abuse
3700 Forest Drive
Suite 300
Columbia, SC 29204
(803) 734-9520

South Dakota
Department of Human Services
700 Governor's Drive
Pier South D
Pierre, SD 57501-2291
(605) 773-4806

Tennessee
Department of Mental Health
  and Mental Retardation
Alcohol and Drug Abuse
  Services
706 Church Street
Nashville, TN 37243-0675
(615) 741-1921

Texas
Commission on Alcohol and
  Drug Abuse

720 Bracos Street
Suite 403
Austin, TX 78701
(512) 463-5510

Utah
Department of Social Services
Division of Substance Abuse
120 North 200 West
4th Floor
Salt Lake City, UT 84103
(801) 538-3939

Vermont
Agency of Human Services
Department of Social and
  Rehabilitation Services
Office of Alcohol and Drug
  Abuse Programs
103 South Main Street
Waterbury, VT 05676
(802) 241-2170

Virginia
Department of Mental Health
  and Mental Retardation
Division of Substance Abuse
109 Governor Street
8th Floor
P.O. Box 1797
Richmond, VA 23214
(804) 786-5313

Washington
Department of Social and
  Health Service
Division of Alcohol and
  Substance Abuse
12th and Franklin
Mail Stop OB 21W
Olympia, WA 98504
(206) 753-5866

West Virginia
Department of Health and
  Human Resources
Office of Behavioral Health
  Services
Division on Alcoholism and
  Drug Abuse
Capital Complex
1900 Kanawha Boulevard East
Building 3, Room 402
Charleston, WV 25305
(304) 348-2276

Wisconsin

Department of Health and
Social Services
Division of Community
Services
Bureau of Community
Programs
Office of Alcohol and Drug
Abuse
1 West Wilson Street
P.O. Box 7851
Madison, WI 53707-7851
(608) 266-2717

Wyoming

Alcohol And Drug Abuse
Programs
451 Hathaway Building
Cheyenne, WY 82002
(307) 777-7115

U.S. TERRITORIES AND POSSESSIONS

American Samoa

LBJ Tropical Medical Center
Department of Mental Health
Clinic
Pago Pago, American Samoa
96799

Guam

Mental Health & Substance
Abuse Agency
P.O. Box 20999
Guam 96921

Puerto Rico

Department of Addiction
Control Services
Alcohol and Drug Abuse
Programs
Avenida Barbosa
P.O. Box 414
Rio Piedras, PR 00928-1474
(809) 763-7575

Trust Territories

Director of Health Services
Office of the High
Commissioner
Saipan, Trust Territories
96950

Virgin Islands

Division of Health and
Substance Abuse
Becastro Building
3rd Street, Sugar Estate
St. Thomas, Virgin Islands
00802

CANADA

Canadian Centre on
Substance Abuse
112 Kent Street, Suite 480
Ottawa, Ontario
K1P 5P2
(613) 235-4048

Alberta

Alberta Alcohol and Drug
Abuse Commission
10909 Jasper Avenue, 6th
Floor
Edmonton, Alberta
T5J 3M9
(403) 427-2837

British Columbia

Ministry of Labour and
Consumer Services
Alcohol and Drug Programs
1019 Wharf Street, 5th Floor
Victoria, British Columbia
V8V 1X4
(604) 387-5870

Manitoba

The Alcoholism Foundation of
Manitoba
1031 Portage Avenue
Winnipeg, Manitoba
R3G 0R8
(204) 944-6226

New Brunswick

Alcoholism and Drug
Dependency Commission
of New Brunswick
65 Brunswick Street
P.O. Box 6000
Fredericton, New Brunswick
E3B 5H1
(506) 453-2136

Newfoundland

The Alcohol and Drug
Dependency Commission
of Newfoundland and
Labrador
Suite 105, Prince Charles
Building
120 Torbay Road, 1st Floor
St. John's, Newfoundland
A1A 2G8
(709) 737-3600

Northwest Territories

Alcohol and Drug Services
Department of Social Services
Government of Northwest
Territories
Box 1320 - 52nd Street
6th Floor, Precambrian
Building
Yellowknife, Northwest
Territories
S1A 2L9
(403) 920-8005

Nova Scotia

Nova Scotia Commission on
Drug Dependency
6th Floor, Lord Nelson
Building
5675 Spring Garden Road
Halifax, Nova Scotia
B3J 1H1
(902) 424-4270

Ontario

Addiction Research
Foundation
33 Russell Street
Toronto, Ontario
M5S 2S1
(416) 595-6000

Prince Edward Island

Addiction Services of Prince
Edward Island
P.O. Box 37
Eric Found Building
65 McGill Avenue
Charlottetown, Prince Edward
Island
C1A 7K2
(902) 368-4120

Quebec

Service des Programmes aux
Personnes Toxicomanie
Gouvernement du Quebec
Ministere de la Sante et des
Services Sociaux
1005 Chemin Ste. Foy
Quebec City, Quebec
G1S 4N4
(418) 643-9887

Saskatchewan

Saskatchewan Alcohol and
Drug Abuse Commission
1942 Hamilton Street
Regina, Saskatchewan
S4P 3V7
(306) 787-4085

Yukon

Alcohol and Drug Services
Department of Health and
Social Resources
Yukon Territorial
Government
6118-6th Avenue
P.O. Box 2703
Whitehorse, Yukon Territory
Y1A 2C6
(403) 667-5777

Further Reading

General

Berger, Gilda. *Drug Abuse: The Impact on Society*. New York: Watts, 1988. (Gr. 7–12)

Cohen, Susan, and Daniel Cohen. *What You Can Believe About Drugs: An Honest and Unhysterical Guide for Teens*. New York: M. Evans, 1987. (Gr. 7–12)

Musto, David F. *The American Disease: Origins of Narcotic Control*. Rev. ed. New Haven: Yale University Press, 1987.

National Institute on Drug Abuse. *Drug Use, Drinking, and Smoking: National Survey Results from High School, College, and Young Adult Populations, 1975–1988*. Washington, DC: Public Health Service, Department of Health and Human Services, 1989.

O'Brien, Robert, and Sidney Cohen. *Encyclopedia of Drug Abuse*. New York: Facts on File, 1984.

Snyder, Solomon H., M.D. *Drugs and the Brain*. New York: Scientific American Books, 1986.

U.S. Department of Justice. *Drugs of Abuse*. 1989 ed. Washington, DC: Government Printing Office, 1989.

The Addictive Personality

Anthony, J. C., and J. E. Helzer. "Syndromes of Drug Use and Dependence." In *Psychiatric Disorders in America*, edited by L. N. Robins and D. A. Regier. New York: Free Press, 1989.

Cox, W. M., ed. *Identifying and Measuring Alcoholic Personality Characteristics*. San Francisco: Jossey-Bass, 1983.

Fingarette, Herbert. *Heavy Drinking: The Myth of Alcoholism as a Disease*. Berkeley: University of California Press, 1988.

Mendelson, Jack H., M.D. *Alcohol: Use and Abuse in America*. Boston: Little, Brown, 1985.

Vaillant, G. E. *The Natural History of Alcoholism*. Cambridge: Harvard University Press, 1983.

Glossary

addictive behavior behavior that is excessive, compulsive, and destructive psychologically or physically

anorexia nervosa an eating disorder characterized by a pathological fear of weight gain leading to faulty eating patterns, malnutrition, and excessive weight loss

augmenter a person who magnifies the intensity of a stimulus

bulimia a constant and abnormal craving for food, often accompanied by dependence on emetics (drugs that induce vomiting) and laxatives to eliminate the food consumed

cognition the ways in which people think about and organize themselves

delta alcoholism a type of alcoholism in which the afflicted person does not drink large amounts on a single occasion but cannot abstain from alcohol for even a brief amount of time without suffering from withdrawal symptoms

delusion a belief that has no basis in reality

denial refusal to acknowledge or admit something, such as a problem or an addiction

depressant drugs drugs that depress the central nervous system; used to help people block out unpleasant thoughts and anxieties and reduce tension

depression a sometimes overwhelming emotional state characterized by feelings of inadequacy and hopelessness and accompanied by a decrease in physical and psychological activity

ectomorph an individual with a light build, originally from W. H. Sheldon's description of different body types and how they relate to personalities

Electra complex the term often used to describe the Oedipus complex when it occurs in a female

endomorph an individual with a heavy, fatty body build, originally from W. H. Sheldon's description of different body types and how they relate to personalities

euphoria a mental high characterized by a sense of well-being

extroverted being concerned with what is outside the self

factor analysis the process of transforming statistical data into variables and categorizing them

field dependence psychologists' term for the condition of people who rely on external stimuli to form their perceptions

field independence psychologists' term for the condition of people who rely on internal stimuli to form their perceptions *introverted*   being concerned with one's own mental life

locus of control   the factor that determines decisions for a person. If a person is in control of him- or herself, he or she has an internal locus of control. If a person requires outside forces, such as fate or religion, to make decisions, he or she has an external locus of control

manic   affected with or characterized by mania—excitement manifested by disorganization of behavior and elevation of mood

mesomorph   an individual with a husky, muscular build, originally from W. H. Sheldon's theory of body types and how they relate to personalities

moderate   avoiding extremes of behavior or expression

morphine   opium's principal psychoactive ingredient, which produces sleep or a state of stupor; it is used as the standard against which all morphinelike drugs are compared

Oedipus complex   the positive libidinal feelings that a male child develops toward his mother and that may be a source of adult personality disorders if left unresolved

paranoia   an abnormal tendency toward irrational suspiciousness of others and delusions of persecution

perceptual   referring to the ways in which people see and interpret the world around them

pharmacology   the study of drugs and their effects on living organisms

physical dependence   an adaptation of the body to the presence of a drug, such that its absence produces withdrawal symptoms

psychoactive drug   a drug that alters mood and/or behavior

psychoanalysis   a theory about how psychological disturbances develop; also, a technique for treating these disturbances

psychological dependence   a condition in which the drug user craves a drug to maintain a sense of well-being and feels discomfort when deprived of it

psychopathology   the study of psychological and behavioral disturbances

psychosomatic   relating to both mind and body

reducer   a person who minimizes the intensity of stimuli in stimulus intensity modulation experiments

Rorschach test   a test invented by the Swiss psychiatrist Hermann Rorschach. People taking the Rorschach test are given cards stained with inkblots and are asked what the inkblots look like and why the image reminds them of these associations

stimulant drug   any drug that increases behavioral activity

stimulus   something that incites feeling or activity

stimulus intensity modulation   experiments involving psychological mechanisms that come into play in a person's reaction to physical stimuli, especially unpleasant ones

thematic apperception test   a test in which people are given cards with drawings of objects or people on them and are asked what events are taking place on the cards. Invariably the person taking the test will unconsciously incorporate him- or herself into the story

tolerance   a decrease of susceptibility to the effects of a drug due to its continued administration, resulting in the user's need to increase the drug dosage in order to achieve the effects experienced previously

withdrawal   the physiological and psychological effects of discontinued usage of a drug

Index

W. Miles Cox, Ph.D., received his degree in psychology from the University of South Carolina. He was a National Research Service Award postdoctoral fellow in Alcohol/Alcoholism at Oregon Health Sciences University and Indiana University. Currently, he is a professor of psychology and director of the Drug Information Program at the University of Minnesota.

Paul R. Sanberg, Ph.D., is a professor of psychiatry, psychology, neurosurgery, physiology, and biophysics at the University of Cincinnati College of Medicine. Currently, he is also a professor of psychiatry at Brown University and scientific director for Cellular Transplants, Inc., in Providence, Rhode Island.

Professor Sanberg has held research positions at the Australian National University at Canberra, the Johns Hopkins University School of Medicine, and Ohio University. He has written many journal articles and book chapters in the fields of neuroscience and psychopharmacology. He has served on the editorial boards of many scientific journals and is the recipient of numerous awards.

Solomon H. Snyder, M.D., is Distinguished Service Professor of Neuroscience, Pharmacology and Psychiatry at the Johns Hopkins University School of Medicine. He has served as president of the Society for Neuroscience and in 1978 received the Albert Lasker Award in Medical Research. He has authored *Drugs and the Brain, Uses of Marijuana, Madness and the Brain, The Troubled Mind,* and *Biological Aspects of Mental Disorder* and has edited *Perspectives in Neuropharmacology: A Tribute to Julius Axelrod.* Professor Snyder was a research associate with Dr. Axelrod at the National Institutes of Health.

Barry L. Jacobs, Ph.D., is currently a professor in the neuroscience program at Princeton University. Professor Jacobs is the author of *Serotonin Neurotransmission and Behavior* and *Hallucinogens: Neurochemical, Behavioral and Clinical Perspectives.* He has written many journal articles in the field of neuroscience and contributed numerous chapters to books on behavior and brain science. He has been a member of several panels of the National Institute of Mental Health.

Jerome H. Jaffe, M.D., formerly professor of psychiatry at the College of Physicians and Surgeons, Columbia University, is director of the Addiction Research Center of the National Institute on Drug Abuse. Dr. Jaffe is also a psychopharmacologist and has conducted research on a wide range of addictive drugs and developed treatment programs for addicts. He has acted as special consultant to the president on narcotics and dangerous drugs and was the first director of the White House Special Action Office for Drug Abuse Prevention.

0 0 6 3 9 9 8

ADDICTIVE PERSONALITY

COX